AE Mind

"Better Memory Now" Series Presents:

HOW TO REMEMBER NAMES AND FACES

Master the Art of Memorizing Names and Faces with Over 500 Memory Training Exercises of People's Faces

By Luis Angel Echeverria
Memory Master Champion

Memory Coach with AE Mind at
www.AEMind.com

D1478900

YOUR GIFTS

As a bonus, you'll be the first to get my latest **Free Memory Training Videos** and Content to help you with your ongoing continued memory improvement education!

I have also included an updated version of my Picture Associations for Male and Female Names to help you Remember Names much more quickly! :

Download Here:
www.RememberNamesBook.com/Master

Get Access Now at:
www.RememberNamesBook.com/Master

LEARN MORE / CONTACT

Learn more about Luis Angel's "Better Memory Now" programs and other Memory Training material for Professionals, Students, Memory Athletes, and Everyone Else, by going to:

www.AEMind.com

<u>SOCIAL</u>

YT: Youtube.com/aemind
FB: Facebook.com/aemind1
IG: ae.mind
Twitter: @aemind

Email: Support@AEMind.com

TESTIMONIALS

What others say about Luis Angel and The AE Mind: Better Memory Now System

HEATHER CAMPBELL
Coldwell Banker in Huntington Beach, CA

"We were so happy to have Luis here today. He met with me and my husband, we're the brokerage owners, as well as about 30 of our realtors to help us improve our memory's. **We really need to work on remembering our clients' names and interesting things about them to make that personal connection and Luis was great. He had so many great ideas for visualization, helpful memory techniques..."**

JEANNINE
ReMax Masters in Downey, CA

"Today we had the pleasure of having Luis Angel with the Memory Seminar... **gave us ideas on how to remember names**, **and strategies that really will help us with our business.**"

DORINDA
ReMax Omega in Arcadia, CA

"I had an **Awesome Training Session with Luis Angel** this morning on **Memory Techniques**. We learned extensively how to decide **where to put the information, how to remember the information, and how to recall it. I highly recommend his memory training."**

Nathan Brais
Director of Student Life at Coastline College

"I just want to give a big shout out to Luis Angel Echeverria. Thank you so much for coming to our event. You're awesome, with a close to 500 students and staff here. You did 2 memory workshops for us, which the students were really impressed by, and I really appreciate you also doing our keynote address.

Luis is engaging and he's also great with students. He has a very energetic presence and I highly recommend him for any of your school events that you may be having for high school or for college group."

DANNY BELTRAN
AE Mind Memory Athlete and Student at UC Irvine.

"Joining the AE Mind team has been one of the best decisions I've ever made. ***I was taught to memorize so many things without having to tear my head apart and it is so useful in academics,*** *not to mention* ***everyday life.*** *Luis is a great mentor and coach. Without him I wouldn't be in the position I'm in now. Thanks Luis for everything!"*

KASSANDRA CEJA
AE Mind Memory Athlete and Student at UC Irvine

"Meeting Luis and joining the AE Mind Team has been a great experience. Not only did we get the chance to compete in the memory competition in New York, but we also learned skills that helped us memorize material for our academic courses. ***We also got the opportunity to learn strategies that would benefit us with our future careers.*** *Being on the team we learned lots of skills, it opened our doors to many new opportunities, we got to meet many inspiring people, and it was overall one of the best decisions I have made."*

THANK YOU

GOD!
Mom!

Find out the incredible impact that these individuals and several others have made in my life, in the
Thank You Section

CONTENTS

ABOUT LUIS ANGEL

- 1st Memory Master Champion on FOX's Superhuman
- **Founder** and Main Memory Coach at AE Mind | Accelerated Empowered Mind
- **Competed** in the USA Memory Championship
- **Was the Youngest American** to Compete in the World Memory Championship with TEAM USA
- **Memorized** a 120 Digit Number in 5 Minutes
- **Coached the AE Mind Memory Team** to a 1st Place Medal in the Numbers event at the USA Memory Championship
- **Started AE Mind Memory Clubs** in Los Angeles High Schools and in Universities such as UC Irvine and UC Santa Barbara.
- **Speaker** for Schools, Organizations, and Companies to help students and professionals have a "Better Memory Now"
- **Author and Creator of the AE Mind:** *Better Memory Now* **Series**

CONTRIBUTION

As someone who grew up in government-subsidized housing, on food stamps, and in an area with a lot of gang activity (never participated, but witnessed a lot of it around him), Luis Angel knows what it's like to have to go through struggle in life.

That's why Luis Angel loves contributing to help make the lives of those in need better in whichever way that he can.

GIVE BACK TUESDAY
Along with Living Waters and Countless of Amazing Volunteers, Luis Angel helps feed the homeless and families in need every Tuesday in the City of Santa Ana in Southern California.

FEED FAMILIES EVENT

Luis Angel has also partnered with Dion Jaffee, Bell High School, and several friends who donate to the cause to Feed Families every year for Thanksgiving!

A portion of the proceeds from the AE Mind Better Memory Now Live Events, Courses, and Books goes to continuing our Contribution Efforts!

Thank You In Advance for Your Contribution to the Cause!

FOREWORD

**Ron White, 2x USA Memory Champion and Founder of
www.RonWhiteTraining.com**

Luis Angel is one of the rising stars in teaching and demonstrating memory. Over the last few years I have watched him develop into a trusted resource for those looking to learn memory while at the same time honing his own memory skills to competition level.

I've been teaching memory training for 23 years and **I have not seen anyone else come along in the last 23 years that has the drive, ambition, knowledge of memory and talent in teaching that Luis does.**

As a 2x USA Memory Champion, there is no doubt I will enjoy watching Luis compete in memory tournaments for years to come and take home medals. More importantly, **I know Luis will be teaching many people to use and develop their memory to a level they never imagined before.** It was an honor to partner with Luis on a recent memory training video and I enjoyed his friendly and effective teaching style.

Building relationships is key to success in life and **remembering names is key to building relationships.** Using the techniques Luis teaches, I taught a CEO to remember the names of hundreds of his employees. His staff was impressed when he knew the names of everyone that worked in his company, all the way down to the janitors.

People don't care how much you know until they first know how much you care.

I can't think of a more crucial skill for a business person or anyone who wants to achieve more, than remembering names and building relationships.

Imagine if you set a goal to remember the names of 100 new people in the next 12 months. What would that do for your career opportunities, friendships and relationships? Using the techniques that Luis Angel lays out in this book, that is an incredibly attainable goal. That is less than 2 names a week!

In reality you could easily learn the names of 300-500 new people this year with the memory techniques in this book.

Regardless of the size of your goal, I hope that you do set a goal to remember the names of the people you meet this year. You will be amazed at how easy connections and conversations become when you show others the respect of remembering their name.

I knew Luis was committed to memory improvement when he road on a bus from LA to Dallas to learn the memory techniques at a memory seminar that I was having. I was impressed by his commitment to learning and I know he has put that same commitment into this new book on memory improvement and teaching you how to remember names and faces with ease.

Practice these techniques and watch your memory power skyrocket!

-Ron

Learn more about Ron White's Memory Improvement Products, Services, and Events at: www.RonWhiteTraining.com

The secret of getting
ahead is getting started

-Mark Twain

Intro

WHAT'S YOUR NAME AGAIN?

WHAT'S YOUR NAME AGAIN?

Hello Jenna!

Or is it Emily? Mindy? Maybe your name was Anthony?

I'm sorry, can you please remind me of your name again?

Oh, that's right! I knew that. I'll make sure to remember it next time.

Now I know that this has never happened to you, right?

You meet someone new and the next time you run into that individual, you tend to not be able to accurately recall his or her name.

Well, if the above has happened even once before, then this book is perfect for you. I'm going to show you how to be able to memorize people's names with ease!

Being Able to Easily Memorize Anyone's Name is literally an art form.

The best way to memorize someone's name is to paint a very creative and elaborate picture on their face or body. Of course I don't mean to actually take out your paintbrush, paint holder, and all of the colors of the rainbow and start brushing the paint on the person's face. They might not be too fond of that. Unless of course you're at a championship sports game where that individual wants their entire body painted in their team colors. Otherwise, let's just stick to creating a mental picture in your mind.

I'm going to give you the Key To Memorizing Anything, Right Now, including but not limited to Someone's Name.
Here you go...

The Key to Memorization... *Drum Roll Please...* is...

VISUALIZATION!

Done.

You now know the secret that all of the top memory athletes from around the world know in order to memorize a lot of information in a short period of time.

Hold on a minute.

First, let's answer the burning question that you have right now in your mind:

"Luis Angel, you mean to tell me that there are guys and gals who call themselves 'Memory Athletes?'"

Yup. And I am actually one of them.

I am one of a few thousand memory athletes who literally sit down and memorize a bunch of random information such as playing cards, numbers, vocabulary words, and even Names and Faces in a competitive setting.

I know that this is not an actual, physically "athletic" sport. As a matter of fact, the only athletic things that we do are, stretching our necks from looking down at a sheet of paper while we memorize everything that's on it, or using our finger muscles to shuffle through a deck of cards and memorize it in under a minute. I'll get into my story and how I got into this field of memory athleticism, in a bit.

Before that, let's go ahead and answer the real important question here, and that is, "How does this whole visualization process work with name memorization?"

I'm glad that you asked.

It's quite simple. Whether we're memorizing a deck of cards or names and faces, we turn everything that we want to memorize into a picture and store it on a mental location.

In the case of names, this is actually the number one most requested "song" from the audience members at my Live AE Mind Seminars and Events.

They say, "DJ Angel, can you please play the 'How to Remember Names' jam?"

My response is, "Of course I can!"

Whether you're at a large conference meeting hundreds of people or you're at the grocery store talking to the cute girl/guy behind you and you exchange names, this one tip alone will help you out tremendously.

How do we apply the principle of visualization to the idea of memorizing names?

If you apply this next tip with every single person that you meet, I guarantee that you will be able to remember their names much more easily and recall their names when it really matters.

Turn the person's name into a picture and associate it with that person somehow.

To really demonstrate the power of the "how to" of the memorizing names technique, let me go ahead and share a quick story.
I was recently at a real estate office meeting where I did my memory improvement presentation for realtors and then promoted the AE Mind: Better Memory Now for Professionals Event. I did two demonstrations where I memorized and recalled a random 40 digit number (I can do a lot more if I have extra time) and as many of the audience members' names as I had time to meet.

The individuals at these presentations are always impressed by those memory demos and the fact that after I do the awesome feats, they also learn how in the blue wide world I was able to memorize so much information in a short period of time.

At the real estate office meeting, I taught the realtors the system that I'm going to be teaching you here in this book. Several of the audience members ended up investing in their further education by taking advantage of the offer for my BMN Live Event.

Here is the part that makes this entire learning process worthwhile.

One of the young ladies that signed up for the event came that following month. As I saw her walking into the room, I immediately said without hesitation, "Brenda! It's so awesome to see you again!"

This simple act of greeting her by her first name made her give me a look of pure astonishment. She couldn't believe that while it had been an entire month since I had last seen her, I was still able to recall her name with ease.

Ask yourself this: "How valuable would adding this skill of memorizing and recalling anyone's name with ease be in my life?"

I bet that the answer to that question would be along the lines of "Extremely Valuable," especially when you want to build long-term connections and relationships with the people that you are meeting.

In **How to Win Friends and Influence People**, Dale Carnegie says the following, "Remember that a person's name is to that person the sweetest and most important sound in any language."

Remember how you felt when someone that you met weeks or months ago walked up to you and called you by your name? You felt special, right? You felt like you mattered, didn't you? You felt like this person actually cared about you, correct?

This is exactly how others feel when you call them by name a week later, a month later, a year later, or even just a few minutes after you meet them.

Now let's flip the script.

Isn't true that sometimes the following happens when you meet someone for the first time?

You go up to someone, shake hands, and exchange names. After several minutes of talking and conversing, your heart starts beating a little faster when they say, "It was nice talking to you 'Jane/John/Insert Your Name Here.' I hope to connect with you again sometime in the near future."

In that moment, the little gerbils in your brain kick it into overdrive trying their hardest to retrieve this person's name. They're scattering through different regions of your brain, turning over mental files left and right searching for that extremely important piece of information, their name.

After a few seconds of trying to find the name with no luck, you finally say, "It was nice meeting you too." At this point, you walk away with the thought that you hope you never run into that person again because you forgot their name and don't want to experience the pain of embarrassment.

I want to help you out here so you never experience that pain again!

Let me elaborate more on the technique and give you an example.

What I am doing when I'm memorizing a room full of people's names or even just one person that I meet at the park (Yes. Instead of going to the club, I do go out to the park to meet people. I have a Husky and I take her out for walks; she's a great conversation starter) is that I first ask myself "What stands out about this individual?" If it was the fact that they have a mole on the side of their face (like I do), then I would use that as a **LOCATION** to store the name.

Now, when the person gives me their name, I immediately convert it into an image and attach it to the location. So if the individual was a young lady named Alyssa, I would **VISUALIZE** A Lasso being wrapped around the Mole and see myself yanking off the mole by tugging on the lasso.

Once I have that visual representation created in my mind, I would then bring back the image a few times throughout the conversation and **REVIEW** the story association that I created with the name and this young lady.

Disclaimer If the Visual Association that you created can be taken as offensive by the person that you are talking to, *DON'T* actually tell them that story out loud. You might break the rapport that you have built. What you want to do is **See the Image in your Mind.**

That's it!

If you start doing this in your everyday interactions with the people that you meet, you will see that your ability to remember and recall someone's name will dramatically increase!

HOW DID I GET STARTED?

So what makes me qualified to be teaching you these memory and focus improving methods?

A few years ago, I was at the lowest point mentally than I've ever been in. You see, I grew up a pretty happy and cheerful person. Through the ups and downs that life brings (and trust me, there were a lot of downs), I've always tried to keep a smile on my face.

Then a few months before turning 21, I hit the highest threshold of pain that I could endure. It wasn't physical pain but mental pain.

I remember sitting on a bench at Catalina Island, crying my eyes out overlooking the Pacific Ocean's blurry waters. I remember feeling very depressed for the first time ever in my life. I'd never had this feeling before. This weird emotion and state of mind was foreign to me. All that I could think about was all of the bad stuff that was going on in my life.

WORK MEMORY PROBLEMS

At that time, I was working at a satellite TV company. I would go around from house to house installing cable. It was fun at times but mainly it was extremely challenging for me.

Why is that you're asking?

Well, I was doing a very poor job all around at the different tasks that I had to do. I was constantly losing my tools, which was costing the company money. I was extremely slow at my jobs. I kept forgetting what I had to do next. I kept calling my trainer to help me out with basic things, such as where to point the satellite dish to find the correct signal.

I remember many times having to pull out my tall ladder, carry it to the side of a customer's home, climb up the ladder, and right before I started drilling to install the satellite dish, I would realize that I had forgotten a tool down in the van.

I would climb back down the ladder, walk over to the van, open the side door, look around, and stop for a moment to ponder on another realization.

What do you think that was?

I had completely forgotten what I needed to get and at times why I was even in front of the van in the first place. I would then make that long walk back to the ladder, climb it, and then it would hit me, I needed to get the wrench. Then in mind, I would keep repeating, "wrench, wrench, wrench..." the entire way back to the van.

There were even times when I would say this for the first few steps and then my mind would wander off into lala land again.

When I got to the van for the second time, you guessed it, I would have to repeat that entire process because I had once again forgotten what I needed to get.

Has this ever happened to you?

A time where you needed to get something from let's say a room and when you walk over to that room, you look around and wonder why you are in this location.

You knew that you were supposed to get something but have no clue what or why.

This used to happen to me constantly. I was at the verge of losing my job. My supervisors were checking up on me constantly to make sure that I did my tasks properly and didn't skip any steps or forget any of my tools.

HOME MEMORY PROBLEMS

At home, my mom would ask me, "¿Mijo. Que comistes ahora?" (that's Spanish for "Son, what did you eat today?") I would look up and stare out into space wondering if I had even eaten that day. I could have had the biggest grand slam breakfast that morning, ate an entire buffet, and I would still be asking myself "Did I eat today?"

SCHOOL MEMORY PROBLEMS

The other big contributing factor to me not being at an optimal state of mind was the fact that I wasn't doing so well in school.

In high school, I had a 1.0 GPA my freshman year. I spent my summers throughout my high school career repeating freshman level courses just to be able to graduate. If it wasn't for my English Teacher giving me a D in that class my senior year, I would not have graduated. I actually had an F all the way through that last semester.

I was literally praying to God, as I sat with my cap and gown at our senior graduation, that they would call out my name. All of my family was in attendance in the stands waiting for the announcement, "Luis Angel Echeverria Carrion, come on up and get your diploma." If the students failed any of the core classes their senior year, then those students wouldn't be able to walk up on stage. They would have to sit through the duration of the graduation ceremony and see everyone else get called up.

The administrators didn't tell you ahead of time if you were going to officially graduate or not. You just had to wait and see. When they finally did call my name, I was ecstatic and relieved at the same time. I saw my report card the next week and sure enough, it showed a D next to Ms. Solano's English Class. So if you're reading this, Ms. Solano, I want to thank you for allowing me to walk the stage on graduation.

After it was all over, I was glad that I was going to go into college with a fresh start.

How do you think I did when I started my first semester in college?

I started getting straight As, right?

Final answer? Well, I know that you were rooting for me; however, that is incorrect.

I actually continued the same pattern that I had throughout high school. I continued to not be able to focus, pay attention, and always forget what I had "learned."

I dropped out of class after class. They placed me on probation and even kicked me out for a semester because of how poorly I was performing in the classroom.

All of this just kept adding up and stacking on top of each other.

TURNING POINT

It came to a boiling point that day at Catalina Island. I was out there because the satellite TV company used to send me out every few weeks to set up the people from the island with cable.

Well, that morning I had a bad start. I forgot to set my alarm the night before and didn't properly pack everything for the trip to the island. When I did wake up, the ferry that goes to the island was going to leave in less than an hour. I quickly got dressed and raced (carefully of course) in the company van over to the docking port. I stuffed everything that I needed into my black rolling tub and started to haul it up the stairs over to the ticketing desk. The ferry was about to start rolling back the porting rail for departure. Thankfully they let me board. I let out a sigh of relief before the hour-long journey on our way to Avalon (Catalina's main city).

When I arrived on the island, my first customer picked me up and took me over to his home on the back of his golf cart. The roads aren't that wide in the city and gas is pretty pricey out there, so almost everyone drives golf carts.

After doing my site survey to make sure that I was going to be able to complete my job, I went over to my big black tub of goodies. I opened up the heavy container and started looking around for my drill. Guess what I did? I left it back in the van. The van was back in the port, across the Pacific Ocean.

Okay fine. I'll just cancel this job and go to my next two homes on the route list.

Well, at each one of those, I also forgot key equipment that I needed to complete the tasks.

I just cost the company a lot of money again in sending me out there for nothing.

So there I was sitting on that bench. I said, "That's it! No more! This is the last time that this will happen to me." I was tired of constantly forgetting things.

SOLUTION TO MY MEMORY PROBLEMS

When I got back home, I remembered that my friend Dion had gone to a personal development conference that I couldn't attend because of work.

At this conference, there was a gentleman up on stage who memorized a few hundred of the audience members' names and was recalling them all from memory. He then taught those in attendance how he did it.

When Dion and a few other friends came back from the event, the only speaker that they were bragging about was this memory guy.

So I called Dion and said, "Hey man, what was that memory guy's name?"

He told me, "His name's Ron White, and he has a memory program that you should check out."

I said thanks and purchased the program within minutes. It normally takes people a month to go through it, and I did the entire memory course in 3 days.

Why?

Because I didn't want to feel the pain that I felt of not being able to remember things that I should be able to recall with ease.

I started to apply the techniques that I learned from Ron to my studies at school and at work. I went from failing my classes in college to getting straight As in the last several semesters. At work, I went from nearly getting fired to getting a promotion and becoming the youngest technician at the office to hold the new position that I had.

MEMORY ATHLETE and COACH

I then went on to compete in memory competitions and even became the Youngest American to compete in the World Memory Championship in London, England.

It was awesome!

I saw that this was helping me out tremendously in every area of my life, and I decided to pursue my passion of helping others. I enjoyed the reaction that others experienced not when they saw me doing these amazing memory feats, but when I taught them how to do it and use it in their lives.

Students were using it to learn faster. Professionals were using the memory techniques to remember their customers' names. Memory athletes were using the skills to compete in memory competitions.

In 2014, I took a team of students to the USA Memory Championship. This team of students had never previously learned the memory techniques. With a few months of training, I flew with 8 students from Los Angeles to New York to compete against schools that had been doing this for many years prior to us entering the competition.

How do you think that we did against them?

Well, **the AE Mind Memory Team from Los Angeles was the 1st Place winner in the numbers event!**

My students went on to get the gold medal in an event that normally takes schools years of training to win in.

Above that, all of the seniors in that team are now attending high-ranking universities in California. Some went to UC Irvine and one went to UC Santa Barbara. It was amazing to see how far they had come; we started in high school, and now I'm working with them to run college memory clubs in their schools.

PASSION!

So as you can see, I'm not just a guy off the street who read an article online about memory improvement and thinks he can wave a magic wand to make you a memory genius.

I've put in the work. I've trained my memory for thousands of hours, and I continue to train every day.
I continue to go to high schools and colleges to work with students and teachers. I continue to go to professional offices and events to work with individuals who want to take their career or business to the next level by tapping into their full mind's potential. I continue to work with memory athletes who want to compete in memory competitions. I still also teach just everyday individuals who want to remember something as simple as a list of grocery items that they have to pick up when they go shopping.

This is My Passion!

I love teaching others how to improve their memory, and I'm looking forward to working with you to help you be able to quickly **Remember Names and Faces**!

GETTING STARTED RIGHT

This is going to be a partnership.

I have gone to many seminars and read many books where the speaker or author does a one-way interaction with the audience and expects them to be experts in that topic when they're done.

That's not how accelerated learning works.

At every single one of my seminars or events, whether I'm teaching a group of thousands of people or just doing a one-on-one training, the way that I teach is very interactive.

It's very hands on.

This is the only way that you're going to learn this quickly and truly have an AE Mind (Accelerated and Empowered Mind)!

So I have separated this entire book into five sections. I will start you off with going into the AE Mind Memory System and progress into doing several Name Games.

These Name Games consists of names and faces. There are over 500 faces for you to practice with, and I will be there to help you throughout the process.

GRAMMAR

Just to get this out of the way right now, I did have a proofreader go over the entire book before publishing it. I applied the majority of her grammar suggestions to this book. Some of them I didn't use because I know that you will benefit more from the way that I have structured certain phrases in the book than what traditional English grammar rules dictate. This was done with the intention of maximizing the information that you learn in the shortest amount of time.

Many times throughout the book, you will see words capitalized that would normally be marked as an incorrect use of capitalization in a college paper. The reason for those capitalized words is so that you say them with an inflection in your mind. This will make those words or phrases get cemented deeper into your long-term memory, much more quickly.

REVIEW

I know that if you go through the exercises in this book, that you will see a major improvement in your ability to Remember Names.

I love seeing the transformation that people go through when they learn this system, and I would be extremely grateful if you helped contribute to that transformation.

When you get a chance, if you could take about a minute or two to go to the **Remember Names Book Page** and leave a Review, you will truly be helping to improve the lives of thousands of people who struggle with remembering names.

Thank You in Advance!

Other than that, let the show begin!

Enjoy, and Much Success on your journey to have an AE Mind!

(Copyright/Legal Info Because all of the images used in this book are licensed images, meaning we purchased the rights to use the images in this book, we must let you know that the images used in this book cannot be reproduced, stored in a retrieval system, or transmitted in any form or by any means, electronic, mechanical, photocopying, recording, without our direct consent. If you would like to get the licenses to use these images, please go to: www.ShutterStock.com.)

Thank you for understanding.

Now let's have some fun!

Section I
THE AE MIND SYSTEM

SECTION I – THE AE MIND SYSTEM

You will be learning the 3 Simple Steps that it takes to memorize anything and how you can apply the AE Mind System to Remembering Names and Faces with Ease!

The AE Mind - Memorizing Names System

1. Location
A place to store the name

2. Visualize
Convert the name into an image and visualize it on the location

3. Review
Go over the Visual that you created in order to store it into your long-term memory.

Let's start off by going over the Location aspect of this process and what exactly would make for a great storage space.

"Tell me and I forget. Teach me and I Remember. Involve Me and I Learn."
-Benjamin Franklin

Chapter 1

LOCATION

Awesome!

You've made it to the first chapter; the starting line; the foundation.

This is the first step to us being able to memorize anyone's name with ease.

Let's jump right in.

Again, my name is Luis Angel, and I am your memory coach.

I meet new people every day, as I'm sure you do as well. The first thought that goes through my mind when I first meet a new person is, "What stands out about this individual?"

I then quickly lock in on that location and prepare for the name exchange. I'll get into how to take the name and associate it to the location in the next chapter. Also, I make sure to quickly glance at the location that stood out to me and not do a glaring stare the entire time I'm looking at the person I just met. It would creep out the person that you are meeting for the first time if you just stared at one spot on their face during the duration of your first encounter.

PRACTICE THIS

A tip that I can share is to start practicing seeing someone with your peripheral view. This means that you sort of defocus your eyes and notice what you see in your surroundings while continuing to look straight ahead.

Practice this right now. Go ahead and find something near you that stands out. Now look at that item and while keeping your gaze straight ahead, notice everything that's near and around this thing. What do you see on the left, right, up, down, near, and far side of this object?

Great!

This is exactly what I would recommend that you do when you're choosing something that stands out about the individual that you are encountering. With your eyes locked onto the other person's eyes, I want you to use your peripheral view to see a distinguishing facial feature that stands out.

If it's a challenge for you to do that right away, then take a quick glance at the feature that stands out and before focusing back on the individual's eyes.

Here are examples of locations that you can use:

BEST

These are the best facial features to look out for when choosing a location on a person's face, because they rarely change. Unless of course that person gets some type of surgery done. At that point, it won't be your fault if you have a hard time recognizing who they are the next time you meet them. But other than that, I would recommend to stick with these spots as your primary choices for locations.

It's like in football, when you're the quarterback and have multiple wide receivers to choose from. In each play, you always have your first option and if that player isn't open, then you default to your other receivers.

These features should be your first options when selecting a location:

- Forehead
- Eyebrows
- Nose
- Lips
- Mole
- Wrinkles/Lines
- Dimples
- Chin
- Cheeks
- Eyes - Color/Shape

OKAY

These features/accessories are what I consider to be "okay" locations. The reason why I give them that rating is because they are not always constant and can often change.

- Hair Style
  - Curly
  - Straight
  - Multi-Colored
  - Bangs
  - Short
  - Spiky
  - Bald
- Facial Hair
  - Beard
  - Goatee
  - Sideburns
  - Mustache
- Normal Use Glasses
- Teeth

Be careful with choosing these as your storage locations for the names. They can often change or be removed. The person might have curly hair one day and straight the next.

If they're wearing sunglasses, don't use that as a location. If you know that the glasses that they are wearing are prescription glasses, then you can use them if you can't find another unique feature to use as a location.

As for facial hair, well, let me give you an example.

I was taking improv classes a few years back. I memorized all of my classmates' names using this technique. One of them was Broussard. The way that I memorized his name was by imagining myself leaving a bruise on his full-grown beard.

Broussard and I would chat during breaks and we worked really well together during scenes. Whenever we did a scene together, the audience would absolutely love it.
One day a "new" guy came into the room. He had a familiar face,

but no one could remember how we knew him. During break, he said hi to me and I said hi back then quickly looked away. It felt weird having this gut feeling that I had seen this guy before, but I couldn't put my finger as to where I knew him from.

Finally, he started talking and the first thing that he said to everyone was, "It feels funny having a bald face." We all instantly remembered that this "new" guy was actually Broussard. He had shaved off all of his facial hair. That was his key feature and without it, no one could recognize him.

We all laughed about it and I even told him what I created as a memory trigger to remember his name. I normally don't tell people the images that I create, especially if it involves me imagining myself punching that person in the face so hard that it leaves a bruise.

So use "Okay" locations with caution.

TEMP

These are locations of last resort. You only want to use these as temporary locations, especially if you're meeting a lot of people at once and don't have enough time to pick out a facial feature.

- Clothes
    - Shirt color or design
    - Sweater
    - Blouse
    - Tank top
    - Short sleeve
    - Long sleeve
    - Suit and tie
    - etc...
- Jewlery
    - Necklace
    - Earrings
    - Nose Rings
    - etc...
- Temp. Glasses
    - Sun Glasses
- Makeup
    - Lipstick
    - Eye shadow
    - Face Blush

Again, these are just temporary holding locations. If you used their shirt as a location, more than likely this individual will not be wearing the same clothes the next time that you bump into him or her, so that location might not be the most ideal if you want to recall their name a month from now.

Store the picture for their name on this location only if time is limited and make sure to relocate the image on a facial feature that really stands out to you when time permits.

An example of this would be if you're at a networking event and are being introduced to 5 people that you're meeting for the first time. You know that you will have some extra time to have a one-on-one interaction with each one of them later in the day or night and want a quick way to store their name on a temporary location.

What you want to do is first ask yourself, "What stands out about this individual?"

If you can't quickly get a "Best" facial feature that stands out but instead notice that this person is a young lady with large looped earrings, then it is okay to use one of the earrings as a "Temp" location. Store the image on there quickly and then move on to the next individual.

Once you have been introduced to each person and let's say that you visualized all of their names using a Temp Location, when you have that one-on-one interaction, make sure to focus on a facial feature that really stands out about that individual.

During the one-on-one with the young lady with the earrings, you notice that she has a mole right below her left eye. What you want to do at that point is move the image that you created for her name onto the new location by Visualizing it Vividly interaction with that mole. If her name is Sandy, you can picture sand being poured all over her mole.

EXERCISE

Here is an exercise to start noticing these locations:

Whenever you are out and about, maybe at the grocery store, walking to a local restaurant, or at the gas station, start to Ask Yourself, "What Stands Out About This Individual?"

See if you can spot two or three facial features that really stand out about this person. Does he or she have a thin shaped nose, high cheekbones, dimples, moles, thin or plump lips, eye color – essentially anything that you can use as a mental location to store the image of that person's name. You don't even have to ask them for their names, this exercise is meant for you to start noticing the facial features that POP out at you.
In the next chapter, we're going to get into the real meat and potatoes of how to memorize someone's name.
I will give you the first NAME GAME where you will be able to put what you learned in this chapter into practice!

Let's do it!

Chapter 2

VISUALIZE

Remember that the Key to Memorization is Visualization.

You have to become a Creative Storyteller when you are memorizing anything, especially Names.

Let's say that you meet this individual

The first question you want to ask is, "**What Stands Out about this Individual?**"

- Gray Hair
- Goatee
- Teeth
- Blue Tie *Temp*

Let's go ahead and choose his teeth for illustration purposes.

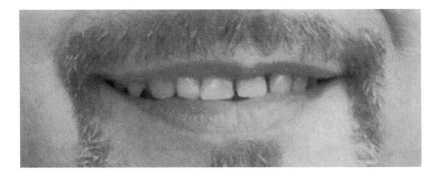

So now that we have a location picked out, how do we actually memorize that person's name?

This is where the essence of the visualization process begins. We take the name and convert it into a picture. We then take that picture and imagine it doing something on the location that we chose for that individual.

How do we convert the name into a picture?

We start with a question,
"What does this name remind me of?"

This gentleman's name is Paul.

Paul reminds me of a **Ball**.

You then take the Picture for the Name and Visualize it doing something on the location.

You essentially create a story out of these two things.

The story could go something like this:

You were playing tennis with Paul and you hit one of the tennis balls really hard towards his face. The ball then got stuck in the middle of his teeth in the gap. Now every time Paul smiles, you see a tennis ball.

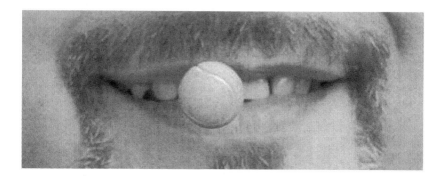

I want you to add as many senses as you possibly can to this story:

- Sight
- Smell
- Sound
- Feel
- Taste

What do you **see** when this happens?

Are there any **smells** that you can add to this story? Maybe you go check up on Paul to see how he's doing and his breath smells.

Are there any **sounds** associated with this story? Paul at first lets out a huge scream and then starts laughing uncontrollably because he has a Tennis Ball stuck on his teeth.

How does it **feel**? Imagine yourself feeling the teeth and trying to take the tennis ball out.

Can you add the sense of **taste** to the above image? Maybe imagine Paul tasting the tennis ball and saying "yummy!"
I know that this might seem like a lot of work just to remember a person's name, however, you have to trust that your brain is very powerful, creative, and can do this in an accelerated manner. Because guess what? It can!

I do this process with everyone that I meet. Many times I create an entire vivid story in milliseconds because right after shaking one person's hand, I have to shake and meet someone else.

The more that you practice this process of Visualizing and associating someone's name to a Location on their face, the easier this is going to get.

You are essentially learning a new language here.

You're learning the language of converting names into pictures.

The beautiful part about this is that once you convert someone's name into a picture, you will always use that picture for any new person that you meet with the same name.

The next time that you meet a "Paul" you will imagine a "Ball" doing something on a facial feature that stood out to you.

This is similar to when you were first learning the names for everyday objects. A Spoon is Always A Spoon. You don't call it something different every time that you ask for it at a restaurant. Like can you please bring over a xygraeb. The waiter is going to look at you like you just made up that word. (I actually did just make it up. I literally looked down at my keyboard and typed a few random letters together.) You learned a long time ago what a spoon looks like and now, no matter what the size or overall shape of that item, it is always a Spoon.

So every time that you meet someone new, for whom you already have a picture representation of their name, go ahead and use it. It will make this entire process much easier.

The most challenging part of this process will be to convert every name into an image. Of course I will make it easy for you because I am going to give you hundreds of images for names.

I have included that list in the back section of this book.

You can also download it here, along with the Remember Names Video Series:
www.RememberNamesBook.com/Master

NAME GAME: 1

Let's go ahead and practice right now with 12 names. I'll give you my picture representation for each one of these names:

#.	Name	=	Picture
1.	Abby	=	A Bee
2.	Al	=	Owl
3.	Angel	=	Angel Wings
4.	Ann	=	Ant
5.	Bridget	=	Bridge
6.	Fred	=	Fred Flintstone
7.	James	=	Chains
8.	Luis	=	Lace (shoe)
9.	Peggy	=	Pegged Leg
10.	Rosa	=	Red Rosa
11.	Teddy	=	Teddy Bear
12.	Wanda	=	Wand

Now those are my picture representations for the names. If one of them doesn't quite resonate with you or you feel that you can come up with a better image, by all means feel free to do that. I learned how to do this from my mentor, Ron White, and I really liked the images that he uses for names. Many of those images, I preferred to use pictures that I felt a stronger connection with. So it's completely up to you whether you want to use the pictures that I have for names or if you want to use your own.

Let's go ahead and put this to the test. How about we take those names from up above and attach them to some faces?
I have both the Name of the Person and the Picture for that Name right underneath the Face.

Go ahead and choose some facial feature that stands out about that individual, then take the image for the name and visualize it doing something on that location.

NAME GAME: 1

Al (*Owl*)	Luis (*Lace*)	Bridget (*Bridge*)
Fred (*Flinstone*)	Peggy (*Pegged Leg*)	James (*Chains*)
Abby (*A Bee*)	Teddy (*Bear*)	Wanda (*Wand*)
Angel (*Wings*)	Ann (*Ant*)	Rosa (*Red Rose*)

Great!

Now that you have all 12 down, let's see how many of those you can recall.

Go ahead and write down the 12 names in the next page.

Don't worry about spelling. If you write down Anne instead of Ann, it is perfectly fine. Unless you're competing in a memory competition where spelling does count, we won't need to focus on that in this book.

NAME GAME: 1

NAME GAME: 1

Whatever the mind of man can conceive and believe, it can achieve.

-Napoleon Hill

ANSWERS FOR NG: 1

#.	Name
1.	Al
2.	Luis
3.	Bridget
4.	Fred
5.	Peggy
6.	James
7.	Abby
8.	Teddy
9.	Wanda
10.	Angel
11.	Ann
12.	Rosa

Score: _____ / 12

How did you do?

Did you get all of them correct? Most of them?

If you missed any, ask yourself "Why?"

Why do you think that you missed that name? Was the visual association not strong enough? Maybe you didn't resonate too well with the image representation that I have for that name. If that's the case, make sure to choose a picture representation for that name that you like.
If you got them all right, congratulations!

You were probably saying, "This was easy!" That could possibly be the case. I gave you some pretty easy names to memorize. You could quickly translate those names into images. Abby is A Bee. Al is an Owl. Those are pretty easy to see.

Now you're probably asking, "What about more complex names like Rebecca or Alexander?"

It's the same process. Rebecca is a Rowing Book. Alexander is a Leg Sander. You take the name and ask yourself, "What does this name remind me of?"

In Chapter 5, I'll give you another tip to help you remember names easier.

Now let's move on to the most important step of this process. This next step is crucial if you want to remember something for a longer period of time.

The next chapter is all about the importance of Reviewing!

Chapter 3

REVIEW

At the last USA Memory Championship, I memorized a 114 digit number in a matter of minutes. I perfectly recalled that number on a separate blank sheet of paper. Ask me today if I can recite that 114 digit number back to you right now.

The politically correct answer is, "Nope."

I don't even know what the first digit was. I know that it was a number between 0 and 9, but I won't be able to specifically tell you what that number was.

Is it because I'm not truly a memory master? Is it because this memory technique doesn't work? No and no.

This memory system is powerful!

Let me prove it to you.

Next time you see me, ask me to say the first few hundred digits of Pi out loud both forwards and backwards.

I'll say sure. Close my eyes. Take a deep breath in through my nose and exhale softly out through my mouth as you see my shoulders start to slump down for a bit before coming back up (this is a Relaxation and Focus exercise that I go over in my **Better Memory Now book**). I will then stick my arms out a bit and start doing some Tony Stark type of movement with my hands swiping left and right and scribbling into thin air as I say:

3.14159265358979323846264338327950288419716 9... so on and so forth.

Or ask me what the atomic number for any element on the periodic table of elements is, and I'll instantly give you the answer.

47 is Silver, Beryllium is 4, Carbon is 6, the 50th element is Tin…
Again, this is all from memory.

Now I don't do that just to brag or show off, I do it to show you the
power of the memory techniques when applied in the manner that
I teach you.

So what is the difference between what I memorize in a memory
competition and what I learn in an education setting?

The difference is obvious. I actually care about the information
and want to hold on to it for a longer period of time when it comes
to learning educational material. When I'm training for a memory
competition, I want to erase the information that I memorized as
quickly as possible so that I could reuse the mental locations for
another set of numbers, cards, or vocabulary words. - I teach how
to do these things and much more in the Better Memory Now
book.

The key element for anyone to be able to retain information for a
long period of time is to Review!

So in order to forget the information that I memorized in a
competition setting, I just don't review that info past the recall time
in the competition.

When I want to remember something such as math formulas,
vocabulary words, or someone's name, I make sure to review that
information in a spaced period of time.

Meaning I'll use the Visualization Technique to Memorize the
information the first time around and then I'll review the info later
that day, the next day, and a few days afterwards as well.

When it comes to names, if you don't review the names of the
people that you meet, then you are more likely to either forget
their name or have trouble recalling it quickly.

When you review information, you're telling your brain that this is
important and that it should store it into its long-term memory.

NERD ALERT

I'm going to get a little technical here. So if you are brave enough to go through the next few pages, by all means do so, especially if you would like to get a better understanding into the importance of reviewing.

If you want to skip this part and just want to get the overall premise, here it is:

>> Reviewing = Long Term Memory. <<

In the book "**The Other Brain**," Dr. Douglas Fields talks about how when we review something, brain cells called glial cells help support the neurons to fire off much more quickly the next time that you want to retrieve that information. More specifically, these glial cells shoot off something called myelin onto the neurons when they send electrical signals down the axons and then the terminals shoot off neurotransmitters to the receiving end of another neuron (the dendrites).

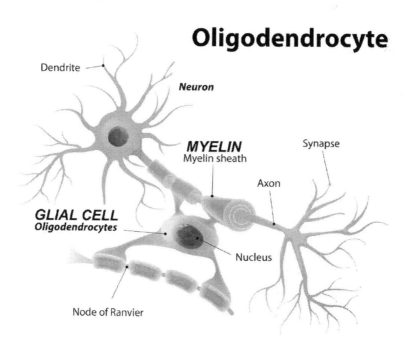

Oligodendrocyte

Dendrite

Neuron

MYELIN
Myelin sheath

Synapse

Axon

GLIAL CELL
Oligodendrocytes

Nucleus

Node of Ranvier

Let me explain the importance of this process through a metaphor.

As you know from reading the Intro section, I used to work for a satellite TV company. My job was to install the customer's cable and make sure that everything was running smoothly before I left. Meaning they needed to be able to see their favorite TV channels and shows before it was time for me to pack up and go to my next job.

The way that they received a pretty HD picture on their TV set was because the cable connected to the back of the receiver box was getting a digital signal coming from the satellite dish that converted another signal coming from the actual satellites floating hundreds of miles up in space.

Amazing, I know!

So what carries this electrical signal from the satellite dish, through the cable, and onto the receiver?

It's a copper wire only about a few millimeters thick. It's probably as thick as an unfolded paperclip.

So why is it that the actual cable that you see hooked up to the back of your TV cable box is much thicker than what it should be?

This is because in order for the signal to flow smoothly and in a quick manner from one end to the other without getting any signal loss, the copper wire needs to be wrapped with insulation. There are actually several layers of insulation, as you see below.

I've had to go to hundreds of troubleshooting service calls at customers' houses during my stint as a cable installer, and one of the biggest problems was that the dog had chewed up the cable. They had cut through the insulation, leaving the copper cable exposed and not allowing the electrical signal to reach the cable box.

Now with that knowledge in your brain, let's apply this to how our neurons work.

Imagine that the axon, which carries the electrical signal, is the copper cable. The insulation is the myelin that wraps around the axon.

Without any or perhaps just a thin layer of myelin, the neurons don't fire off as effectively and efficiently as they should. However, when you repeatedly fire off those neurons by reviewing the information that you want to memorize and learn, the glial cells pick up on that and send myelin to wrap around the axon.

Again, **Reviewing = Long Term Memory.**

> **As an FYI,** Did you know that when they were looking at Albert Einstein's brain, the neuroscientists couldn't see any size difference between his brain and an average brain?
>
> What they did see that was different was the amount of white matter in his brain. The white matter is the myelin that wraps around the neurons. He had a lot more white matter than the average human brain.
>
> Albert Einstein was known to visualize or create thought experiments in his mind when he wanted to solve a problem. This is just something to consider when going through this process of Visualizing in order to Memorize.

MEMORY TIP

Something that I still do on a regular basis is journaling.
I have journals for my different areas of life. I have one for
business, one for memory training, one for my daily review, and
one for social improvement.

In the social improvement journal, I write down the names of all of
the people that I met that day. I jot down a quick note of a facial
feature that stood out to me. At the end of the week, I'll do a quick
review of everyone that I met and even some key points that we
talked about during our conversation.

Now you don't have to go out and buy 10 different journals right
now for every area of your life. You don't even have to go out and
get a journal to write down the names of the people that you meet.

What I would recommend for you to do is to review the people's
names that you meet for that day before going to sleep. This could
happen by just seeing their faces in your mind's eye and
visualizing the story that you created with the picture for their
name and the facial feature that stood out.

In Chapter 13, I'll give you another memory tip to help you with
this review process.

The key is to review the name so that your brain can retrieve it
much more quickly the next time that you see that person.

Section II

BEGINNER OF NAMES

SECTION II – BEGINNER OF NAMES

In the next several sections, we are going to get to work to turn you into a Master of Names!

I am going to be giving you non-stop practice sheets for you to strengthen your brain's neuronal connections with this new language that you are learning of turning names into pictures and visualizing that image on a person's face.

This section will start off with some easy names and as we progress through the book, the tasks are going to be a little more challenging. I'll be giving you more names to memorize in the same period of time and I'll even teach you how to memorize last names.

Remember that the Sweetest Sound to Anyone's Ear is their Name!
- "How To Win Friend's and Influence People" by Dale Carnegie

Chapter 4

WARM UP

We'll start off with two easy name games in this chapter.

I've given you my picture representations for the names; all that you have to do is go over them and use those pictures to store them on a facial feature for the corresponding face.

Quick Reminder

The AE Mind Memory System

1. Location
What Stands Out About This Individual?

2. Visualize
What Does This Name Remind Me of?
Store the picture on the location.

3. Review
What did I picture on this individual's location?

Let's Do This!

NAME GAME: 2

The first 12 names and pictures for those names are as follows:

#.	Name	=	Picture
1.	Brad	=	Bread
2.	Brent	=	Bran Cereal
3.	Cannon	=	Cannon
4.	Felix	=	Felix the Cat
5.	Harper	=	Harp
6.	Mary	=	Wedding Veil
7.	Mike	=	Microphone
8.	Nicole	=	Nickel
9.	Pearl	=	White Pearl
10.	Ron	=	Man Running
11.	Ruth	=	Babe Ruth Chocolate
12.	Tracy	=	Tracing with Pencil

NAME GAME: 2

Tracy	Harper	Ruth
Ron	Brent	Felix
Cannon	Mike	Mary
Nicole	Pearl	Brad

NAME GAME: 2

Faith is taking the first step even when you don't see the whole staircase.

-Martin Luther King Jr.

NAME GAME: 2

NAME GAME: 2

All of these Name Games have the answers in the back of the book. Be sure to check your results once you complete each game!

How did you do with Name Game #2?

Did you get them all right?

Remember to make the visual association very strong and vivid. It will get easier the more that you do this.

NAME GAME: 3

Here's another go at it with 12 new names with their pictures:

#.	Name	=	Picture
1.	Ashley	=	Ashes
2.	Ben	=	Bench
3.	Billie	=	Billy Goat
4.	Claudia	=	Cloud
5.	Jo	=	Sloppy Jo
6.	Jose	=	Water Hose
7.	Leon	=	Lion
8.	Oliver	=	Olive
9.	Paige	=	Page (paper)
10.	Pat	=	Pat with Hand
11.	Phil	=	Gas Pump
12.	Rex	=	T-Rex

NAME GAME: 3

Phil	Jo	Ben
Ashley	Oliver	Paige
Rex	Leon	Claudia
Billie	Jose	Pat

NAME GAME: 3

Two roads diverged in a wood, and I – I took the one less traveled by, And that has made all the difference..

-Robert Frost

NAME GAME: 3

NAME GAME: 3

Remember to Check your answers in the back of the book!

Is this getting pretty easy?

In the next chapter, we're going to start Turning Up the Heat. The names are going to get a little more challenging.

Are you up for that?

The only way to truly master this is to push yourself to do things that challenge you past your comfort zone. That's what my job is here. To push you, but trust me I'll be here to help you along throughout the process

Chapter 5

TURN UP THE HEAT

These next 12 names revolve around another Names and Faces Memory Tip. Let me teach it to you through a story.

Story Time

A few months back, I was going to my first open yoga session at a park in Orange County. I had never been there before and I was lost. I saw a young lady carrying a yoga mat walking towards the direction that I was guessing was where the yoga meet-up was going to be at.

I told her that I was starting to get worried about possibly missing my first yoga session until she showed up. We started talking about yoga and fitness as we made our way down the hill towards the section of the park where the rest of the group was having the yoga session. I then asked her for her name, which she said was "Hilary."

What do you think was my first thought when she said that?

You guessed it!

I said "Like our next President?"

She laughed and we ended up having a conversation about politics the rest of the way down.

(**Side note**: *For those who have already made a judgment as to what my political stance is, I just want you to know that I'm not a Democrat or a Republican. I am an Independent. I just threw that out there to spark a conversation with the young lady*)

Teaching Point

What did I do here?

I used the "**Who Does this Remind Me of?**" Names Technique to create a visual association with this young lady's name.

Hilary reminds me of Hillary Clinton.

If you can't quickly think of an object or even an action for the name, then ask yourself, "Who Does this Name Remind Me of?"

Another example of this was when I was at a bank and the bank teller greeted me. The teller's name was Jordan. We began to have a conversation about Michael Jordan and basketball.

There are two things that happen when you use this method.

1. It is a great way to break the ice and to build rapport by talking about their name.

2. You're building a strong connection with their name and something that you have prior knowledge about, making their name more memorable.

When Tony Robbins teaches others about how to learn anything quickly, he says that the key is to take the thing that is unknown and link it to something that is known.

That's what we're doing with names. We take a name and link it to something that our mind already has a link for.

NAME GAME: 4

Here are some examples of names that remind me of people that I know or know of. You can choose friends, family, or famous people.

Make sure to still ask yourself "What Stands Out About This Person?" when you are choosing a location to store the image representation for the name. Then take the picture that you created and visualize it doing something on that location.

So if the person is Britney and her nose stands out to you, make sure to picture Britney Spears singing to her nose.

#.	Name	=	Picture
1.	Alicia	=	Alicia Keys
2.	Barney	=	Barney & Friends
3.	Bradley	=	Bradley Cooper
4.	Britney	=	Britney Spears
5.	Dakota	=	Dakota Fanning
6.	Homer	=	Homer Simpson
7.	Jenny	=	Jenny (Forrest Gump)
8.	Jordan	=	Michael Jordan
9.	Kim	=	Kim Kardashian
10.	Kobe	=	Kobe Bryant
11.	Minnie	=	Minnie Mouse
12.	Tony	=	Tony Robbins

NAME GAME: 4

Homer	Tony	Barney
Minnie	Kobe	Alicia
Jenny	Dakota	Kim
Britney	Bradley	Jordan

NAME GAME: 4

You miss 100% of the shots you don't take.

-Wayne Gretzky

NAME GAME: 4

NAME GAME: 5

Now go ahead and try it out yourself. Ask yourself "Who Does This Name Remind Me of?"

Remember that it can be a friend, family member, or even a famous person.

Write down the associations for each one of these names in the box below.

#.	Name	=	Picture
1.	Antonia	=	_____
2.	Cynthia	=	_____
3.	Gordon	=	_____
4.	Carlos	=	_____
5.	Julie	=	_____
6.	Katie	=	_____
7.	Linda	=	_____
8.	Marlon	=	_____
9.	Morgan	=	_____
10.	Nick	=	_____
11.	Rodrigo	=	_____
12.	Wallace	=	_____

NAME GAME: 5

Cynthia	Marlon	Linda
Morgan	Katie	Nick
Antonia	Wallace	Rodrigo
Carlos	Julie	Gordon

NAME GAME: 5

Every strike brings
me closer to the next
home run.

-Babe Ruth

NAME GAME: 5

Chapter 6

I'M ON FIRE

So now that we've laid down the foundation for converting names into images, let's kick it up a few notches.

When I'm at the **AE Mind:** *Better Memory Now* **Event**, I always get students asking me, "What about Chinese names, or Japanese names, or Russian names, or any foreign name for that matter? How do we memorize those names?"

Let's imagine that you're the Memory Master here (you will be soon), how would you respond to that question?

Exactly, you would say that the Key To Memorization is Visualization!

We convert those names into pictures as well.

How?

Some can be a little trickier than others, however, all you have to do is use your imagination and you'll be able to easily convert the name into an image.

As a reminder, please be sure to leave us a review on the Remember Names Book page where you purchased this from, so that we can continue to help out others in need of being able to memorize names and faces more effectively! Thank you very much!

NAME GAME: 6

Here are some names that I've converted into pictures for you to practice with.

#.	Name	=	Picture
1.	Ashoka	=	Ashes Coca (Cola)
2.	Diarmad	=	Diaper that's Mad
3.	Dmitry	=	Dime Tree
4.	Hajni	=	Hat Knee
5.	Hiyori	=	Yorki Waving Hi
6.	Jihoon	=	Gel Hen
7.	Madhu	=	Mad Hoof (Horse)
8.	Seoyeon	=	Seal Yawn
9.	Tatsuki	=	Tattoo of Key
10.	Yong	=	Yoyo Gong
11.	Yuki	=	U shaped Key
12.	Zheng	=	Zebra Singing

NAME GAME: 6

NAME GAME: 6

Eighty percent of Success is showing up.

-Woody Allen

NAME GAME: 6

NAME GAME: 6

I know that this was a little bit more challenging.

You were probably able to get the image right but maybe not the name exactly correct. That's because you're not used to seeing or hearing that name.

However the more that you use this system, the easier that it is going to be for you to quickly translate the name into a picture and the picture back into the name.

NAME GAME: 7

Now here are a few more names to practice with. I'll mix in some names that you would normally hear with some foreign names. Go ahead and convert these names into images.

#.	Name	=	Picture
1.	Amir	=	_____
2.	Firdaus	=	_____
3.	Khan	=	_____
4.	Wook	=	_____
5.	Hinata	=	_____
6.	Tirto	=	_____
7.	Bruno	=	_____
8.	Willie	=	_____
9.	Evan	=	_____
10.	Scarlett	=	_____
11.	Aaliyah	=	_____
12.	Latoya	=	_____

NAME GAME: 7

Amir	Bruno	Wook
Latoya	Khan	Evan
Tirto	Firdaus	Aaliyah
Willie	Hinata	Scarlett

NAME GAME: 7

I am not a product
of my circumstances.
I am a product of
my decisions.

-Stephen Covey

NAME GAME: 7

You did a Great Job in this section!

You have graduated from the **Beginner of Names** Section on to the Novice of Names Section!

In the next Section, we're going to start going into more names and faces per session and you're going to start doing more of the names to pictures conversion to start getting your brain used to the process when you meet people on a regular basis.

You are learning a lot! Pretty soon you'll be a
Master of Names!

Section III

NOVICE OF NAMES

SECTION III – NOVICE OF NAMES

As we progress through the next few Name Games, you will notice that I'm going to give you more names and faces to memorize per session. It's all part of the process to help you become a Master of Names!

If you want to challenge yourself even further, see if you can set a time limit to look at the names and faces in each Name Game!

Set a timer of 5-10 minutes to memorize the names on the faces and then turn to the recall sheets to see how many you can get in that time frame.

"It is in your moments of decision that your destiny is shaped."
-Tony Robbins

Chapter 7

I'VE GOT IT!

Another memory tip to help you with converting names into pictures is to ask yourself if this name rhymes with anything.

For example:

Jane rhymes with mane, lane, Spain, rain, cane, and brain.

The trick with this tip is to add another link to help remember what the first letter of this name was.

So if you chose Lane to represent Jane, then add a Juice or Jam on that Lane to help you with the recall process.

Because if you use Lane and a week later you run into that person, you will be able to see the image that you associated with her but might have a hard time translating it back into her name.

That's where the extra link comes in. If you see a Juice on the Lane, you know that it started with a J and so her name must be Jane.

This is just something to keep in mind when you're translating these next few names into pictures.

NAME GAME: 8

Let's start with 12 names. I'll help you out with half of the names and you go ahead and do the other half. Team effort here.

#.	Name	=	Picture
1.	Alise	=	_____
2.	Christopher	=	Cross Gopher
3.	Colin	=	Calling (phone)
4.	Emily	=	_____
5.	Fatima	=	_____
6.	Jeanie	=	Genie
7.	Jett	=	_____
8.	Joel	=	(Sloppy) Jo with Elf
9.	Lorraine	=	Low Rain
10.	Peter	=	_____
11.	Stephanie	=	Staff knee
12.	Steven	=	_____

NAME GAME: 8

Fatima	Jett	Jeanie
Joel	Alise	Colin
Stephanie	Christopher	Steven
Peter	Lorraine	Emily

NAME GAME: 8

When you find your "WHY"... You find a way to Make It Happen!

-Eric Thomas

NAME GAME: 8

NAME GAME: 9

Now with these 12 names, I want you to go ahead and create the picture associations for each one of the names.

#.	Name	=	Picture
1.	Arturo	=	_____
2.	Frankie	=	_____
3.	Genece	=	_____
4.	Giuliana	=	_____
5.	Jesse	=	_____
6.	Jesus	=	_____
7.	June	=	_____
8.	Katherine	=	_____
9.	Lauren	=	_____
10.	Nathan	=	_____
11.	Paul	=	_____
12.	Selena	=	_____

NAME GAME: 9

Selena	Paul	Jesse
Genece	Arturo	June
Lauren	Katherine	Frankie
Nathan	Jesus	Giuliana

NAME GAME: 9

Every child is an artist. The problem is how to remain an artist once he grows up.

-Pablo Picasso

NAME GAME: 9

Chapter 8

LAST NAMES TOO?

In the USA Memory Championship, they give us a lot of faces with both first names and last names to memorize.

We have 15 minutes to look at several sheets of these faces with the names and we get one point when we get the first name correct and another point for the last name.

The process is the exact same way.

Two questions to ask yourself with last names:

- **"What does this Last Name remind me of?"**

- **"Who does this Last Name remind me of?"**

NAME GAME: 10

Here are 12 last names, I'll help you with half of them and you go ahead and create the images for the other 6. Ready? Let's do this!

#.	Name	=	Picture
1.	Adams	=	Apple (Adams)
2.	Clark	=	_____
3.	Echeverria	=	Elephant Eating Cheerios
4.	Garcia	=	_____
5.	Gonzalez	=	Going Salty
6.	Harris	=	_____
7.	Jackson	=	Jack (car)
8.	Johnson	=	_____
9.	Jones	=	Jelly on Bones
10.	Lopez	=	_____
11.	Nguyen	=	Nugget
12.	Smith	=	_____

NAME GAME: 10

Jackson	Harris	Johnson
Adams	Gonzalez	Jones
Garcia	Nguyen	Lopez
Clark	Echeverria	Smith

NAME GAME: 10

Find out what it is you want, and go after it as if your life depends on it.

—Les Brown

NAME GAME: 10

NAME GAME: 10

How did you do there?

If this was a little more challenging than it was for the first names, remember to add as many links as possible. When you create the visual association with the location, add as many senses as you can. What do you see, hear, smell, taste, and feel when you visualize the picture of the name with the facial feature?

NAME GAME: 11

In the next Name Game, I'm going to give you 12 last names and 12 first names. Go ahead and convert these next 12 last names into pictures. The first names will be ones that we have already seen in previous NGs.

#.	Name	=	Picture
1.	Baker	=	_____
2.	Brown	=	_____
3.	Coleman	=	_____
4.	Cooper	=	_____
5.	Diaz	=	_____
6.	Hernandez	=	_____
7.	Miller	=	_____
8.	Ortiz	=	_____
9.	Pierce	=	_____
10.	Reed	=	_____
11.	Simmons	=	_____
12.	Warren	=	_____

To memorize both the first name and the last name, you can either:
- Use two separate facial features to link the two names
- Combine both pictures into one story

An example of the 2nd method would be:
Stephanie Diaz = Stepping on Knees with Dice shoes.
I would see that entire image on the location or facial feature for this lady.

Try it out on this Name Game.

NAME GAME: 11

Stephanie Diaz	Rosa Pierce	Alise Baker
Lauren Ortiz	Arturo Brown	Nathan Warren
Jett Simmons	Selena Miller	Peter Hernandez
Linda Cooper	Evan Reed	Bruno Coleman

NAME GAME: 11

The most important days in your life are the day you are born and the day you find out why.

-Mark Twain

NAME GAME: 11

Chapter 9

YES!

Great job so far!

We're making strides. You are doing amazing!

Give yourself a huge high five!

You're probably asking, why am I giving you last names to memorize?

Well, I've done several one-on-one memory training sessions with professionals who meet people all of the time where all that they get is the person's last name.

Or just as a matter of showing respect, they want to call the person by Mr. or Ms. Their Last Name.

At the end of the day, whether you're converting last names, first names, or even vocabulary words into pictures, the act of doing such a thing is helping you sharpen your ax to be able to quickly create these associations on the spot.

Let's practice with a few more Name Games that involve last names.

NAME GAME: 12

Are you ready for 12 new first and last names?

12 First Names

#.	Name	=	Picture
1.	Elise	=	_____
2.	Freddy	=	Fried E (elephant)
3.	Gerald	=	_____
4.	Junior	=	_____
5.	Kay	=	_____
6.	Ken	=	Can
7.	Khloe	=	_____
8.	Lloyd	=	_____
9.	Monica	=	_____
10.	Rafael	=	Roof Elf
11.	Sidney	=	_____
12.	Sylvia	=	_____

NAME GAME: 12

24 Last names

#.	Name	=	Picture
1.	Anderson	=	_____
2.	Bendana	=	Bandana
3.	Briones	=	_____
4.	Delgado	=	_____
5.	Dellis	=	Dallas Cowboys Star
6.	Liu	=	_____
7.	Marino	=	_____
8.	Tapia	=	_____
9.	Thomas	=	_____
10.	White	=	_____
11.	Wilson	=	_____
12.	Zupp	=	Zap (laser)

NAME GAME: 12

Rafael Zupp	Khloe Marino	Freddy Anderson
Sylvia Delgado	Junior Thomas	Elise Bendana
Kay White	Sidney Briones	Monica Tapia
Ken Dellis	Lloyd Wilson	Gerald Liu

NAME GAME: 12

The great aim of
education is not
knowledge but action.

-Herbert Spencer

NAME GAME: 12

NAME GAME: 13

Now Let's try 24 first and last names.

24 First Names

#.	Name	=	Picture
1.	Abigail	=	A Bee Pail
2.	Angela	=	_____
3.	Anthony	=	_____
4.	Bessie	=	_____
5.	Bonnie	=	_____
6.	Cameron	=	Camera
7.	Candice	=	Can Dice
8.	Daniel	=	_____
9.	Deandre	=	_____
10.	Dominic	=	_____
11.	Gustavo	=	_____
12.	Janet	=	Jam Net

#.	Name	=	Picture
13.	Jocelyn	=	_____
14.	Joseph	=	_____
15.	Jude	=	_____
16.	Lindsey	=	_____
17.	Melanie	=	Melon on Knee
18.	Nellie	=	_____
19.	Santino	=	_____
20.	Saul	=	_____
21.	Serena	=	_____
22.	Simon	=	Simon Game
23.	Trevor	=	_____
24.	Zoey	=	_____

NAME GAME: 13

24 Last names

#.	Name	=	Picture
1.	Armstrong	=	_____
2.	Bishop	=	Bishop (chess)
3.	Black	=	_____
4.	Boyd	=	_____
5.	Carrion	=	Carrying Onion
6.	Davidson	=	_____
7.	Duncan	=	Dunking
8.	Fox	=	_____
9.	Hall	=	_____
10.	Knight	=	_____
11.	Larson	=	_____
12.	Leonard	=	_____

#.	Name	=	Picture
13.	Little	=	_____
14.	Palmer	=	Palm
15.	Phillips	=	_____
16.	Ramirez	=	Ram Rice
17.	Rodriguez	=	_____
18.	Scott	=	_____
19.	Stone	=	_____
20.	Tafolla	=	_____
21.	Tran	=	_____
22.	Wagner	=	Wagging
23.	Weber	=	_____
24.	Young	=	_____

NAME GAME: 13

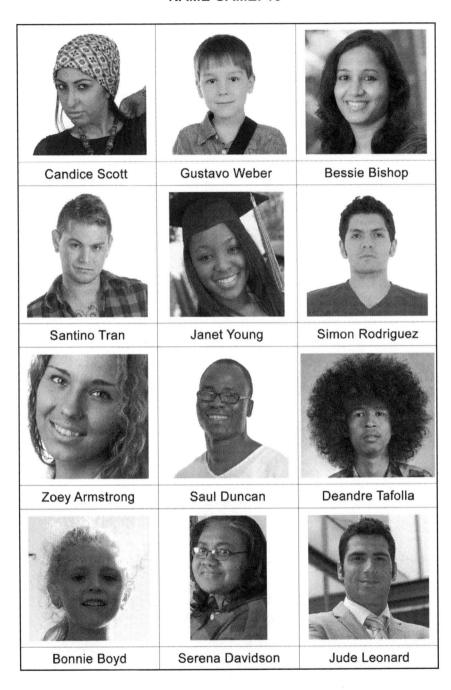

Candice Scott	Gustavo Weber	Bessie Bishop
Santino Tran	Janet Young	Simon Rodriguez
Zoey Armstrong	Saul Duncan	Deandre Tafolla
Bonnie Boyd	Serena Davidson	Jude Leonard

NAME GAME: 13

Lindsey Little	Trevor Fox	Angela Palmer
Nellie Carrion	Cameron Phillips	Dominic Wagner
Abigail Hall	Jocelyn Black	Anthony Ramirez
Joseph Larson	Daniel Knight	Melanie Stone

NAME GAME: 13

> Education is the most powerful weapon which you can use to change the world.
>
> –Nelson Mandela

NAME GAME: 13

NAME GAME: 13

Congratulations!

You have now graduated from the **Novice of Names** onto the Expert of Names Section!

This is where the real fun begins!

The next section will involve you stepping up and taking these names head on!

Are you ready?

Let's Do It!

Section IV

EXPERT OF NAMES

SECTION IV – EXPERT OF NAMES

This is it!

After the first NAME GAME in this section, I'm going to start throwing out no less than 24 names per NAME GAME now!

This section will really push you to be more creative and you will notice yourself getting faster with the conversion process of names into pictures!

What I like to do when I'm memorizing a greater amount of names per session is take a moment to pause after a good chunk of names and review the images of the ones that I have already memorized.

So maybe after the first 6 people, cover the names with your hand or finger and see if you can recall the picture that you created.

Then move on to the next chunk of names.

Bring On The Name Games!

"Imagination is more important than knowledge. For knowledge is limited to all we now know and understand, while imagination embraces the entire world, and all there ever will be to know and understand."
-Albert Einstein

Chapter 10

BRING IT

"Bring It On"

This is what you need to say to any challenge, obstacle, or bump on the road that comes your way!

You are stronger than you think you are. In the case of remembering people's names, trust your brain! Your memory is stronger than you think it is!

Let's Do This!

NAME GAME: 14

#.	Name	=	Picture
1.	Allyson	=	_____
2.	Autumn	=	Autumn Leaves
3.	Betty	=	_____
4.	Elon	=	Iron Man (Elon Musk)
5.	Jacob	=	_____
6.	Jameer	=	_____
7.	Jazmin	=	Jazmin Princess (Disney)
8.	Kevin	=	_____
9.	Maurice	=	_____
10.	Patricia	=	_____
11.	Ryder	=	Motorcycle Rider
12.	Suzanne	=	_____

NAME GAME: 14

Jazmin	Kevin	Allyson
Betty	Jameer	Patricia
Autumn	Jacob	Ryder
Elon	Suzanne	Maurice

NAME GAME: 14

> If you look at what you have in life, you'll always have more.
>
> If you look at what you don't have in life, you'll never have enough.
>
> —Oprah Winfrey

NAME GAME: 14

NAME GAME: 15

#.	Name	=	Picture
1.	Alexander	=	_____
2.	Becky	=	Book Shaped as E
3.	Bethany	=	_____
4.	Bianca	=	_____
5.	Diana	=	_____
6.	Dion	=	_____
7.	Giovanni	=	Cheetos Van
8.	Heather	=	Feather
9.	Irene	=	Eye Ring
10.	Justin	=	_____
11.	Kathy	=	_____
12.	Liz	=	Lizard

#.	Name	=	Picture
13.	Martin	=	_____
14.	Natalia	=	_____
15.	Norman	=	_____
16.	Pablo	=	_____
17.	Paula	=	Ball
18.	Reggie	=	_____
19.	Ryan	=	_____
20.	Sam	=	Uncle Sam
21.	Sean	=	_____
22.	Tanya	=	_____
23.	Terry	=	_____
24.	Vince	=	Fence

NAME GAME: 15

NAME GAME: 15

Alexander	Liz	Dion
Kathy	Terry	Becky
Norman	Reggie	Diana
Natalia	Martin	Giovanni

NAME GAME: 15

> You can't use up creativity. The more you use, the more you have.
>
> —Maya Angelou

NAME GAME: 15

NAME GAME: 15

Chapter 11

CHALLENGE TIME

In the next 2 Name Games, I am going to start weaning you off of me giving you the names in advance. Most of times where you are meeting someone for the first time, you more than likely don't have the luxury of getting the name beforehand.

If you've met someone before with the same name as the new person that you are meeting, well then, you should already have a picture association created for that name.

If this is the first time that you are meeting a person with this name, then you're going to have to unleash everything that we've been working on up to this point and tap into your creativity to create a picture for the name on the spot.

NAME GAME: 16

I am going to give you 18 of the 24 names that you are going to be memorizing.

#.	Name	=	Picture
1.	Adell	=	_____
2.	Astrid	=	Ostrich
3.	Benjamin	=	_____
4.	Carlton	=	_____
5.	Carolyn	=	_____
6.	Carrie	=	_____
7.	Celeste	=	_____
8.	Chad	=	Cheese Pad
9.	Danny	=	_____
10.	Dylan	=	_____
11.	Hector	=	_____
12.	Javier	=	_____

#.	Name	=	Picture
13.	Joshua	=	_____
14.	Kendra	=	_____
15.	Laura	=	_____
16.	Rudolph	=	_____
17.	Sonia	=	Sony (electronics)
18.	Yesenia	=	_____

NAME GAME: 16

Joshua	Yesenia	Astrid
Celeste	Carlton	Adell
Chad	Dylan	Javier
Carolyn	Danny	Carrie

NAME GAME: 16

Benjamin	Kendra	Sofia
Cesar	Ramiro	Jeff
Rudolph	Sonia	Hector
Laura	Velma	Delanda

NAME GAME: 16

Above all else, guard your heart, for everything you do flows from it.

-Proverbs 4:23

NAME GAME: 16

NAME GAME: 16

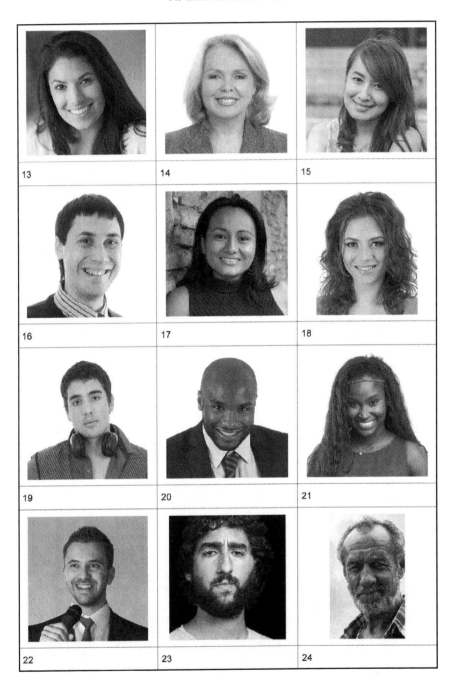

NAME GAME: 17

Now, I am going to give you half of the names that you are going to be memorizing.

#.	Name	=	Picture
1.	Arian	=	_____
2.	Bernadette	=	Burning Net
3.	Celia	=	_____
4.	Ian	=	_____
5.	Jionni	=	_____
6.	Jorge	=	Curious George
7.	Layla	=	_____
8.	Marina	=	
9.	Monique	=	_____
10.	Ramon	=	_____
11.	Randy	=	_____
12.	Victoria	=	Victory (Trophy)

NAME GAME: 17

Mae	Celia	Jionni
Adriana	Rick	Isayas
Monique	Keshawn	Randy
Grace	Christine	Matt

NAME GAME: 17

Victoria	Ramon	Ian
Adrian	Jorge	Valerie
Randal	Oscar	Marina
Layla	Heaven	Bernadette

NAME GAME: 17

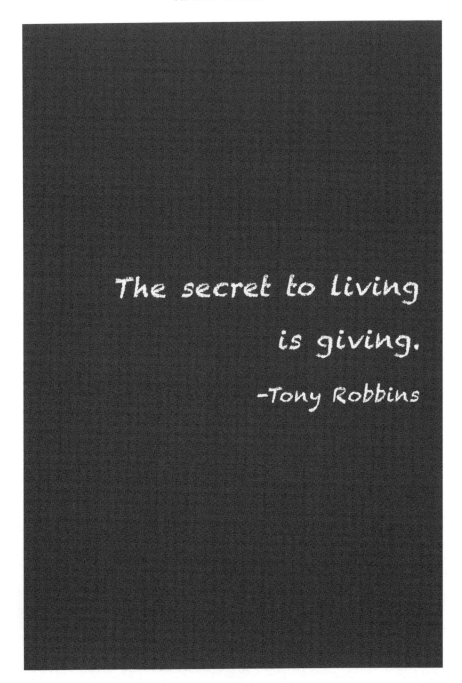

NAME GAME: 17

NAME GAME: 17

13

14

15

16

17

18

19

20

21

22

23

24

Chapter 12

AWESOME!

You are going to love this next Name Game!

Remember to do those chunks of review like I had mentioned earlier. Memorize a few names and then cover up the names to see if you can recall the images. Then move on to the next names.

MEMORY TIP

In my *Better Memory Now* Events, I get a lot of individuals asking me if I can show them how to remember information about the people that they interact with.

Meaning that when they talk to someone, not only do they want to remember what their name is but also what they talked about.

I do show them how I retain facts about someone that I am having a conversation with.

Normally, I bring up a few people up to the front who I use as examples to teach everyone how to memorize names.

I then have the students up on stage tell me a few things about themselves. What do they like to do during their spare time? What do they like to eat? Do they have a pet?

After I get a few points about that person, I pause the session to do a teaching point.

I tell everyone in the room that what I'm doing when I'm getting information about someone is default to the Key to Memorization.

Remember what that is?

It is *VISUALIZATION*!

Our brains learn best in images. They like to SEE the information that you want to retain.

So as the person is telling me something about themselves, I'm SEEING them acting out a story with that information.

So if one of the individuals is a lady and she tells me that she has a pet dog, I might picture her running with a dog on a leash out by the beach.

I might at that point throw in the fact that I have a Siberian Husky and ask her what kind of dog she has.

This adds another link to the chain that we are building to help us remember facts about this person. The more links that you have, the easier that it is going to be for you to tug on this chain and retrieve the information later.

What I'm doing there is linking the unknown, her having a dog, with something that my brain does know, which is that I have a Siberian Husky.

That way, the next time that I run into this person, I can ask how the dog is doing.

Hope that Memory Tip helps you out. Use it! It Works!

Now onto memorizing more names and faces!

NAME GAME: 18

Are you ready for 36 names? Here are 24 of the 36 names.

#.	Name	=	Picture
1.	Ali	=	_____
2.	Amber	=	_____
3.	Beatrice	=	Beats and Rice
4.	Carmen	=	_____
5.	Debbie	=	_____
6.	Desiree	=	Diced Celery
7.	Dwight	=	_____
8.	Floyd	=	_____
9.	Glenn	=	_____
10.	Hope	=	_____
11.	Howard	=	_____
12.	Isabel	=	_____

#.	Name	=	Picture
13.	Jacqueline	=	Jack (car) and Lint
14.	Julian	=	_____
15.	Lemond	=	_____
16.	Lucy	=	_____
17.	Marianne	=	_____
18.	Mario	=	Super Mario
19.	Michael	=	_____
20.	Preston	=	_____
21.	Roxanne	=	_____
22.	Sally	=	_____
23.	Todd	=	Toad
24.	Wayne	=	Rain

NAME GAME: 18

Graham	Dorothy	Jeronimo
Sergio	Ali	Anita
Genesis	Preston	Isabel
Naomi	Kassandra	Todd

NAME GAME: 18

Carmen	Lemond	Desiree
Michael	Beatrice	Floyd
Jacqueline	Glenn	Julian
Jessica	Howard	Kelly

NAME GAME: 18

Wayne	Louis	Debbie
Mario	Hope	Marianne
David	Ricardo	Lucy
Amber	Roxanne	Valentino

NAME GAME: 18

> I have not failed.
> I've just found 10,000
> ways that won't work.
>
> –Thomas A. Edison

NAME GAME: 18

NAME GAME: 18

NAME GAME: 18

Way To Go!

Congratulations on Graduating from the **Expert of Names** Section!

You are now going to have to take this to a whole new level in the Master of Names Section!

Let's Get To It

Section V

MASTER OF NAMES

SECTION V – MASTER OF NAMES

Remember that the Key to Memorization is Visualization.

As a Master of Names, you are going to need to apply everything that we have done up to this point with the previous Name Games!

Spaced Repetition is the Mother of All Skill.

Remember the key principles that we talked about when memorizing names.

The Key to Memorization is Visualization!

All of the Top Memory Athletes apply this principle when they memorize a large amount of information in a short period of time.

The AE Mind Memory System

1. Location
What Stands Out About This Individual?

2. Visualize
What Does This Name Remind Me of?

3. Review
What did I picture on this individual's location?

Let's Get Into It! These Name Games are going to Be Challenging, Fun, and Are Going to Push you to Truly Earn the Title of Being a Master of Names!

"Formal education will make you a living; self-education will make you a fortune."
-Jim Rohn

Chapter 13

I CAN, I WILL, I DID!

We're going to do a few warm up Name Games before I introduce you to the full version of Name Games without pre-knowing the names.

MEMORY TIP

As the title of this chapter goes, I Can, I Will, I Did!, this memory tip is going to revolve around the concept of future pacing.

I learned this from attending multiple mind empowerment events. They always say to state your goals, dreams, aspirations, and visions, in the present tense. As if they're happening right now. This tells your brain that this is a real goal for you to attain, and it will make it easier for you to take action towards that goal.

An example of this would be:

Goal: I want to run a marathon.
Future Paced Vision: It is March 28th, 2016, and I have just completed my first ever LA Marathon in 4 hours flat!

Notice the difference between these two statements. One feels much more distant while the other feels like it's possible and you can obtain it by putting in the work.

Now how do we apply this concept of future pacing to remembering someone's name?

Remember that the 3rd step in the AE Mind Memory System is the most critical step when you want to recall the person's name in the future.

What I normally do once I have created the association of the individual's name with their facial feature that stood out to me is imagine myself interacting with them again sometime in the future.

I visualize myself walking up to them at a networking event and giving them a big hug as I shout out their name. I might then see me bumping into them at the grocery store and greeting them by name again and even asking them about a topic that we had discussed during our first encounter.

I stack multiple future-paced visions in a very quick manner to let my brain know that this person is important to me and that it needs to hold on to his or her name.

Remember that the more links you add to this association chain, the easier it will be for you to recall their name in the future!

As Tony Robbins says, "Spaced Repetition is the Mother of All Skill." In the case of names, Spaced Reviewing is the Father of Perfect Names Recall!

Now let's move onto the first NAME GAME in this section.

NAME GAME: 19

#.	Name	=	Picture
1.	Abel	=	_____
2.	Ada	=	_____
3.	Anilette	=	A Knee with Lid
4.	Axel	=	_____
5.	Beth	=	Bath
6.	Bianca	=	_____
7.	Camilo	=	_____
8.	Candy	=	Candy Cane
9.	Darrell	=	_____
10.	Derek	=	_____
11.	Gilbert	=	_____
12.	Jade	=	_____

#.	Name	=	Picture
13.	Jerry	=	_____
14.	Jim	=	_____
15.	Kaitlyn	=	_____
16.	Karen	=	_____
17.	Madeline	=	Mad Lint
18.	Marcus	=	_____
19.	Mya	=	_____
20.	Nancy	=	Nun Singing
21.	Robert	=	Robot
22.	Sandy	=	Sand
23.	Walt	=	_____
24.	Winston	=	_____

NAME GAME: 19

Kaitlyn	Candy	Gilbert
Madeline	Marcus	Derek
Beth	Walt	Sandy
Mya	Camilo	Jerry

NAME GAME: 19

Bianca	Nancy	Winston
Axel	Abel	Darrell
Jade	Jim	Anilette
Karen	Ada	Robert

NAME GAME: 19

As we look ahead into the next century, leaders will be those who empower others.

–Bill Gates

NAME GAME: 19

NAME GAME: 19

NAME GAME: 20

With this Name Game, I'm going to give you a total of 24 names and faces with 12 names in advance and 12 old and new names. Have fun!

#.	Name	=	Picture
1.	Ariel	=	_____
2.	Athena	=	_____
3.	Bradford	=	_____
4.	Darren	=	_____
5.	Dwayne	=	_____
6.	Edward	=	_____
7.	Felipe	=	_____
8.	Kennedy	=	_____
9.	Lebron	=	_____
10.	Michelle	=	_____
11.	Mikayla	=	_____
12.	Viki	=	_____

NAME GAME: 20

Mikayla	Ariel	Marshall
Daniel	Celeste	Edward
Bradley	Chelsea	Michelle
Ignacio	Yesenia	Felipe

NAME GAME: 20

NAME GAME: 20

I want to put a ding in the universe.

-Steve Jobs

NAME GAME: 20

NAME GAME: 20

NAME GAME: 21

Remember, this is the Mastery Section! I'm going to start giving you Names and Faces without knowing the names in advance.

We'll start it off pretty easy with a NAME GAME of 12 Names and Faces each.

NAME GAME: 21

Nate	Nirey	Alex
Tyrone	Emmanuel	Joy
Gris	Chava	Ida
Bobbie	Lucas	Elizabeth

NAME GAME: 21

You will never do anything in the world without courage. It is the greatest quality of the mind next to honor.

-Aristotle

NAME GAME: 21

NAME GAME: 22

Here are another 12 names. I'll mix this one up with some New and Old names.

Notice how the names that you've already seen before in this book are easier to memorize than the new ones.

That's because your brain has already made the neural connections necessary to bring up the image association for that name come up more quickly.

Again, Spaced Repetition is the Mother of All Skill.

NAME GAME: 22

Hector	Carlos	Eva
Diane	Donna	Karen
Cody	Miriam	Arlene
Luis	Colby	Rajon

NAME GAME: 22

All our dreams can come true, if we have the courage to pursue them.

-Walt Disney

NAME GAME: 22

NAME GAME: 23

Are you ready for one more blind NAME GAME before moving on to the next chapter?

Here are 12 brand new names faces for you to practice with.

Remember to ask yourself,

1. Location = What Stands Out about this Individual?
2. Visualize = What or Who does this Name remind me of?

NAME GAME: 23

Brooklyn	Greg	Priscilla
Christian	Ruben	Marissa
August	Aubrey	Amy
Ted	Jack	Olivia

NAME GAME: 23

Winners make a habit of manufacturing their own positive expectations in advance of the event.

-Brian Tracy

NAME GAME: 23

Chapter 14

OUTSTANDING!

This chapter will feature 2 Name Games of 24 names and one of 36.

Remember to reference the Name's List in the back of the book, if you need help with creating images for the names

Have Fun!

MEMORY TIP

Did you notice how I keep saying "Remember" before reminding you about a key principle?

I often hear people say "Don't forget to XYZ..."
What they don't realize is that they just told that person to Forget XYZ.

Our unconscious mind picks up on the cues that you give it. It's like a search engine. If you feed it a certain keyword, it's going to return queries for that specific keyword.

So instead of telling not only others but also yourself to Not Forget something, do a 180 and tell yourself to Remember XYZ!

You'll be increasing the chances of recalling that information by stating it in a positive manner.

Now let's continue on with our 24th Name Game!

NAME GAME: 24

This NAME GAME will feature 24 names with a mixture of half new ones and half old ones.

NAME GAME: 24

Todd	Vince	Alejandro
Juliana	Anthony	Alice
Heather	Hazel	Iman
Roxanne	Diego	Ariana

NAME GAME: 24

Shelley	Dakota	Rogelio
Leonardo	June	Nelson
Vern	Fred	Joaquin
Ivy	Maggie	Elaine

NAME GAME: 24

Communication – the human connection – is the key to personal and career success.

-Paul J. Meyer

NAME GAME: 24

NAME GAME: 24

NAME GAME: 25

This first NAME GAME will feature 24 names with all new names and faces.

NAME GAME: 25

Kendrick	Irma	Chuck
Veronica	Jane	Andrea
Dennis	Marilyn	Sophia
Ronald	Jason	Moses

NAME GAME: 25

Jared	Morgan	Lydia
Charlie	Melissa	Giselle
Ana	Gabriel	Norma
Molly	Hal	Shawn

NAME GAME: 25

Choose a job you love, and you will never have to work a day in your life.

-Confucius

NAME GAME: 25

NAME GAME: 25

NAME GAME: 26

This NAME GAME will feature 36 Names with a mixture of new and old names.

NAME GAME: 26

Brent	Miguel	Marlene
Briana	Jean	Juan
Jenny	Blake	James
Lupe	Barbara	Omid

NAME GAME: 26

Dante	Jaden	Rowan
Bridget	Jaime	Ashley
Deborah	Mila	Victor
Gil	Rachel	Megan

NAME GAME: 26

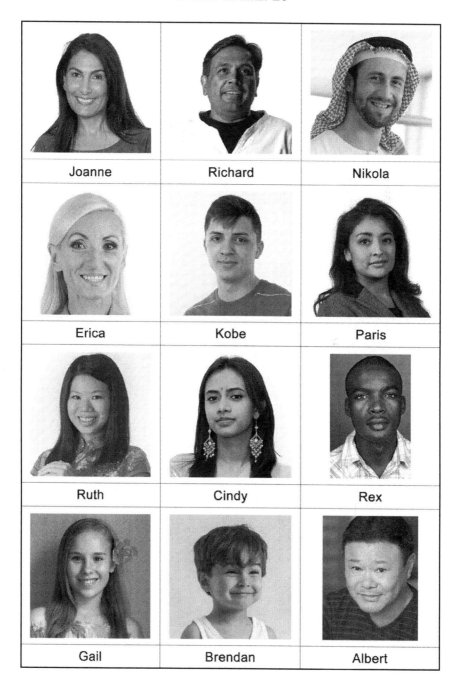

Joanne	Richard	Nikola
Erica	Kobe	Paris
Ruth	Cindy	Rex
Gail	Brendan	Albert

NAME GAME: 26

Discipline is the bridge between goals and accomplishment.

-Jim Rohn

NAME GAME: 26

NAME GAME: 26

NAME GAME: 26

Chapter 15

MASTERY IS MINE!

We have arrived to the final installment of the Name Games!

I will be giving you incremental Name Games here.

Once you accomplish these, you will be considered a Master of Names!

Let's Finish Strong Here!

NAME GAME: 27

This NAME GAME consists of 12 new first and last names.

NAME GAME: 27

Pedro Williams	Margarita Mendez	Alejandra Brooks
Jill Bryant	Hank Peterson	Juliet Nelson
John Gonzalez	Adam Clark	Judy Jones
Kurt Jennings	Brett King	Sky Taylor

NAME GAME: 27

The journey of a thousand miles begins with one step.

-Lao Tzu

NAME GAME: 27

NAME GAME: 27

The journey of a thousand miles begins with one step.

-Lao Tzu

NAME GAME: 28

Here are 24 new first and last names.

Ready?

Let's Do This!

NAME GAME: 28

Sarah Aguilar	Hannah O'neil	Brenda Garcia
Bob Smith	Randolph Lee	Erwin Pope
Maximiliano Carrion	Thomas Reed	Terry Thornton
Annie Mcgregor	Lori Stone	Roberta Frazier

NAME GAME: 28

Natalie Yu	Julia Liu	Ernie Diaz
Jeremiah Barnes	Annabelle Park	Sherry Anderson
Jonathan Hamilton	Walter Mullins	Doris Ortiz
Tyrese Rice	Tansel Cobain	Geogia Ramirez

NAME GAME: 28

He who has a why to
live can bear almost
any how.

-Friedrich Nietzsche

NAME GAME: 28

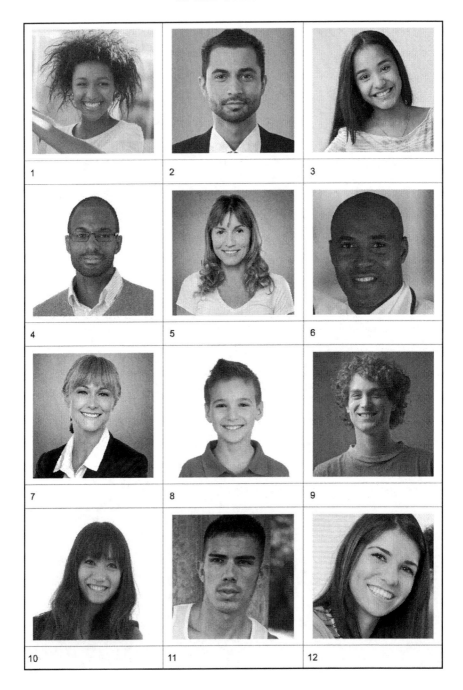

NAME GAME: 28

NAME GAME: 29

You are starting to become a real pro at this. I'm going to give you 36 first names for this Name Game!

NAME GAME: 29

Dmitry	Dawn	Carmelo
Virginia	Landry	Emily
Dirk	Kimberly	Tyson
Sandra	Brian	Judith

NAME GAME: 29

Lexi	Troy	Austin
Selena	Susie	Andre
Gabrielle	Hugo	Alondra
Ajay	Summer	Jesse

NAME GAME: 29

Spencer	Amerlia	Francisco
Luna	Curtis	Alise
Sylvester	Stacy	Shane
Laurie	Michael	Carla

NAME GAME: 29

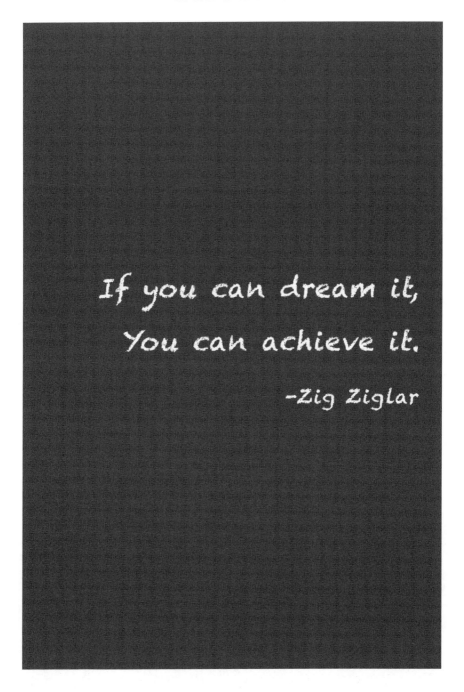

If you can dream it,
You can achieve it.

−Zig Ziglar

NAME GAME: 29

NAME GAME: 29

NAME GAME: 29

NAME GAME: 30

The last NAME GAME will feature 36 first and last names.

Once you go through this, you will be a Master of Names!

NAME GAME: 30

Matthew Lawson	Kyle Russell	Destiny Wells
Eduardo Gasol	Aaron Gore	Lola Santiago
Joy Madison	Chava Huerta	Ashlyn Ly
Catherine Nix	Sharon Fukui	Raymond Vega

NAME GAME: 30

Ling Sun	Wendy Leon	Byron Ford
Alma Jackson	Randy Winter	Amanda Palmer
Debra Phan	Edward Rios	Johnny Kato
Paulina Alford	Isaac Mcfadden	Manuel Ventura

NAME GAME: 30

Esteban Delgado	Jennifer Springer	Feibi Maki
Sue Abrams	Maria Saucedo	Angelica Echeverria
Alan Jordan	Xing Zhu	Chester Bravo
Pamela Lake	Allysa Nguyen	Livan Trejo

NAME GAME: 30

Passion is what gets you through the hardest times that might otherwise make strong (people) weak.

-Neil deGrasse Tyson

NAME GAME: 30

NAME GAME: 30

NAME GAME: 30

Only one who devotes himself to a cause with his whole strength and soul can be a true master.

For this reason mastery demands all of a person.

-Albert Einstein

Congratulations!!
You are now a Master of Names!

Go out and apply what you learned in this Remember Names book to impress others and yourself with this newly acquired skill of Memorizing Names with Ease!

OUTRO

REMEMBER YOUR NAME!

OUTRO

Thank you so much for getting this book and for investing in yourself by mastering the skill of Memorizing and Remembering Names Quickly and Easily!

You are Amazing!

It was my pleasure to serve you throughout this process.

I hope that you liked the journey just as much I enjoyed putting this book together.

I put in a lot of time, energy, and money into making sure that I delivered the best Names book in the industry.

Hopefully now after going through this, you received a lot of value from this book and will continue to practice and sharpen your mind with the techniques taught here!

WHAT'S NEXT?

Keep converting names into pictures and practice this on a daily basis with everyone that you meet. The more that you do it, the easier that it is going to be.

The **AE Mind Memory System** boils down to Three Simple Steps:

1. Location 2. Visualize 3. Review

Remember to do this with everyone that you meet and you will greatly increase your ability to Remember their Names!

Have an Amazing Day!

I hope to see you soon and forever **Remember Your Name**!

ANSWERS

You Are Correct!

Name Game 2	Name Game 3
1. Tracy	1. Phil
2. Harper	2. Jo
3. Ruth	3. Ben
4. Ron	4. Ashley
5. Brent	5. Oliver
6. Felix	6. Paige
7. Cannon	7. Rex
8. Mike	8. Leon
9. Mary	9. Claudia
10. Nicole	10. Billie
11. Pearl	11. Jose
12. Brad	12. Pat
Name Game 4	**Name Game 5**
1. Homer	1. Cynthia
2. Tony	2. Marlon
3. Barney	3. Linda
4. Minnie	4. Morgan
5. Kobe	5. Katie
6. Alicia	6. Nick
7. Jenny	7. Antonia
8. Dakota	8. Wallace
9. Kim	9. Rodrigo
10. Britney	10. Carlos
11. Bradley	11. Julie
12. Jordan	12. Gordon

ANSWERS

Name Game 6	Name Game 7
1. Haini	1. Amir
2. Madhu	2. Bruno
3. Yong	3. Wook
4. Yuki	4. Latoya
5. Ashoka	5. Khan
6. Zheng	6. Evan
7. Dmitry	7. Tirto
8. Tatsuki	8. Firdaus
9. Diamard	9. Aaliyah
10. Jihoon	10. Willie
11. Seoyeon	11. Hinata
12. Hiyori	12. Scarlett

Name Game 8	Name Game 9
1. Fatima	1. Selena
2. Jett	2. Paul
3. Jeanie	3. Jesse
4. Joel	4. Genece
5. Alise	5. Arturo
6. Colin	6. June
7. Stephanie	7. Lauren
8. Christopher	8. Katherine
9. Steven	9. Frankie
10. Peter	10. Nathan
11. Lorraine	11. Jesus
12. Emily	12. Giuliana

Name Game 10	Name Game 11
1. Jackson	1. Stephanie Diaz
2. Harris	2. Rosa Pierce
3. Johnson	3. Alise Baker
4. Adams	4. Lauren Ortiz
5. Gonzalez	5. Arturo Brown
6. Jones	6. Nathan Warren
7. Garcia	7. Jett Simmons
8. Nguyen	8. Selena Miller
9. Lopez	9. Peter Hernandez
10. Clark	10. Linda Cooper
11. Echeverria	11. Evan Reed
12. Smith	12. Bruno Coleman

Name Game 12

1. Rafael Zupp
2. Khloe Marino
3. Freddy Anderson
4. Sylvia Delgado
5. Junior Thomas
6. Elise Bendana
7. Kay White
8. Sidney Briones
9. Monica Tapia
10. Ken Dellis
11. Lloyd Wilson
12. Gerald Liu

Name Game 13

1.	Candice Scott	13.	Lindsey Little
2.	Gustavo Weber	14.	Trevor Fox
3.	Bessie Bishop	15.	Angela Palmer
4.	Santino Tran	16.	Nellie Carrion
5.	Janet Young	17.	Cameron Phillips
6.	Simon Rodriguez	18.	Dominic Wagner
7.	Zoey Armstrong	19.	Abigail Hall
8.	Saul Duncan	20.	Jocelyn Black
9.	Deandre Tafolla	21.	Anthony Ramirez
10.	Bonnie Boyd	22.	Joseph Larson
11.	Serena Davidson	23.	Daniel Knight
12.	Jude Leonard	24.	Melanie Stone

Name Game 14

1. Homer
2. Tony
3. Barney
4. Minnie
5. Kobe
6. Alicia
7. Jenny
8. Dakota
9. Kim
10. Britney
11. Bradley
12. Jordan

Name Game 15

1.	Sam	13.	Reggie
2.	Sean	14.	Natalia
3.	Bianca	15.	Martin
4.	Irene	16.	Giovanni
5.	Heather	17.	Diana
6.	Justin	18.	Dion
7.	Paula	19.	Terry
8.	Ryan	20.	Kathy
9.	Pablo	21.	Alexander
10.	Tanya	22.	Becky
11.	Bethany	23.	Liz
12.	Vince	24.	Norman

Name Game 16

1.	Carolyn	13.	Sofia
2.	Danny	14.	Velma
3.	Dylan	15.	Delanda
4.	Javier	16.	Hector
5.	Chad	17.	Laura
6.	Carrie	18.	Sonia
7.	Carlton	19.	Cesar
8.	Adell	20.	Jeff
9.	Celeste	21.	Kendra
10.	Astrid	22.	Ramiro
11.	Yesenia	23.	Benjamin
12.	Joshua	24.	Rudolph

Name Game 17

1.	Randy	13.	Ian
2.	Adriana	14.	Layla
3.	Monique	15.	Adrian
4.	Grace	16.	Valerie
5.	Matt	17.	Heaven
6.	Christine	18.	Randal
7.	Rick	19.	Jorge
8.	Jionni	20.	Bernadette
9.	Celia	21.	Oscar
10.	Mae	22.	Marina
11.	Isayas	23.	Ramon
12.	Keshawn	24.	Victoria

Name Game 18

1.	Isabel	19.	Julian
2.	Jeronimo	20.	Desiree
3.	Todd	21.	Jessica
4.	Genesis	22.	Howard
5.	Naomi	23.	Glenn
6.	Kassandra	24.	Carmen
7.	Preston	25.	Marianne
8.	Graham	26.	Valentino
9.	Ali	27.	Mario
10.	Anita	28.	Roxanne
11.	Sergio	29.	Wayne
12.	Dorothy	30.	David
13.	Floyd	31.	Debbie
14.	Beatrice	32.	Lucy
15.	Michael	33.	Amber
16.	Lemond	34.	Louis
17.	Kelly	35.	Hope
18.	Jacqueline	36.	Ricardo

Name Game 19

1.	Mya	13.	Anilette
2.	Derek	14.	Ada
3.	Camilo	15.	Karen
4.	Walt	16.	Winston
5.	Beth	17.	Robert
6.	Kaitlyn	18.	Bianca
7.	Marcus	19.	Darrell
8.	Jerry	20.	Nancy
9.	Madeline	21.	Abel
10.	Gilbert	22.	Jim
11.	Candy	23.	Jade
12.	Sandy	24.	Axel

Name Game 20

1.	Isabel	19.	Julian
2.	Jeronimo	20.	Desiree
3.	Todd	21.	Jessica
4.	Genesis	22.	Howard
5.	Naomi	23.	Glenn
6.	Kassandra	24.	Carmen
7.	Preston	25.	Marianne
8.	Graham	26.	Valentino
9.	Ali	27.	Mario
10.	Anita	28.	Roxanne
11.	Sergio	29.	Wayne
12.	Dorothy	30.	David
13.	Floyd	31.	Debbie
14.	Beatrice	32.	Lucy
15.	Michael	33.	Amber
16.	Lemond	34.	Louis
17.	Kelly	35.	Hope
18.	Jacqueline	36.	Ricardo

Name Game 21	Name Game 22
1. Joy	1. Arlene
2. Elizabeth	2. Luis
3. Tyrone	3. Rajon
4. Ida	4. Donna
5. Alex	5. Colby
6. Nirey	6. Cody
7. Lucas	7. Diane
8. Emmanuel	8. Carlos
9. Gris	9. Eva
10. Chava	10. Karen
11. Bobbie	11. Miriam
12. Nate	12. Hector

Name Game 23	
1. Ruben	
2. Olivia	
3. Christian	
4. Greg	
5. Aubrey	
6. August	
7. Priscilla	
8. Jack	
9. Ted	
10. Marissa	
11. Amy	
12. Brooklyn	

Name Game 24

1. Hazel
2. Ariana
3. Juliana
4. Anthony
5. Heather
6. Diego
7. Vince
8. Alejandro
9. Roxanne
10. Alice
11. Iman
12. Todd
13. Nelson
14. Leonardo
15. Vern
16. Fred
17. Elaine
18. Ivy
19. Dakota
20. Maggie
21. Rogelio
22. June
23. Joaquin
24. Shelley

Name Game 25

1. Marilyn
2. Jason
3. Moses
4. Irma
5. Veronica
6. Dennis
7. Chuck
8. Jane
9. Ronald
10. Andrea
11. Sophia
12. Kendrick
13. Melissa
14. Charlie
15. Hal
16. Gabriel
17. Ana
18. Lydia
19. Morgan
20. Shawn
21. Molly
22. Giselle
23. Jared
24. Norma

ANSWERS

Name Game 26

1.	James	19.	Ashley
2.	Brent	20.	Victor
3.	Miguel	21.	Mila
4.	Marlene	22.	Deborah
5.	Briana	23.	Megan
6.	Jenny	24.	Dante
7.	Blake	25.	Gail
8.	Jean	26.	Brendan
9.	Barbara	27.	Cindy
10.	Juan	28.	Albert
11.	Omid	29.	Richard
12.	Dorothy	30.	Erica
13.	Bridget	31.	Nikola
14.	Rowan	32.	Joanne
15.	Gil	33.	Paris
16.	Jaden	34.	Rex
17.	Rachel	35.	Ruth
18.	Jaime	36.	Kobe

Name Game 27

1. Judy Jones
2. Sky Taylor
3. Jill Bryant
4. Brett King
5. Adam Clark
6. Kurt Jennings
7. Juliet Nelson
8. Pedro Williams
9. John Gonzalez
10. Alejandra Brooks
11. Margarita Mendez
12. Hank Peterson

Name Game 28

1.	Roberta Frazier	13.	Tyrese Rice
2.	Bob Smith	14.	Jeremiah Barnes
3.	Hannah O'neil	15.	Doris Ortiz
4.	Maximiliano Carrion	16.	Sherry Anderson
5.	Brenda Garcia	17.	Natalie Yu
6.	Randolph Lee	18.	Julia Liu
7.	Annie Mcgregor	19.	Georgia Ramirez
8.	Erwin Pope	20.	Ernie Diaz
9.	Thomas Reed	21.	Jonathan Hamilton
10.	Lori Stone	22.	Tansel Cobain
11.	Terry Thornton	23.	Annabelle Park
12.	Sarah Aguilar	24.	Walter Mullins

Name Game 29

1.	Dirk	19.	Austin
2.	Kimberly	20.	Hugo
3.	Virginia	21.	Ajay
4.	Brian	22.	Andre
5.	Emily	23.	Alondra
6.	Dawn	24.	Lexi
7.	Carmelo	25.	Curtis
8.	Judith	26.	Sylvester
9.	Sandra	27.	Laurie
10.	Landry	28.	Stacy
11.	Dmitry	29.	Carla
12.	Tyson	30.	Michael
13.	Susie	31.	Luna
14.	Jessie	32.	Francisco
15.	Selena	33.	Amerlia
16.	Troy	34.	Spencer
17.	Summer	35.	Shane
18.	Gabrielle	36.	Alise

Name Game 30

1. Raymond Vega
2. Sharon Fukui
3. Joy Madison
4. Chava Huerta
5. Eduardo Gasol
6. Aaron Gore
7. Kyle Russell
8. Catherine Nix
9. Lola Santiago
10. Destiny Wells
11. Ashlyn Ly
12. Matthew Lawson
13. Manuel Ventura
14. Manuel Ventura
15. Debra Phan
16. Johnny Kato
17. Alma Jackson
18. Paulina Alford
19. Randy Winter
20. Amanda Palmer
21. Edward Rios
22. Byron Ford
23. Wendy Leon
24. Ling Sun
25. Livan Trejo
26. Sue Abrams
27. Maria Saucedo
28. Allysa Nguyen
29. Jennifer Springer
30. Alan Jordan
31. Xing Zhu
32. Feibi Maki
33. Pamela Lake
34. Angelica Echeverria
35. Chester Bravo
36. Esteban Delgado

NAMES LIST

MALE NAMES

Aaden	A Den with Apple	Archer	Bow and Arrow
Aarav	A Ref (referee)	Archie	Archery
Aaron	Air Gun	Ariel	Mermaid
Abdiel	Ape Dealing Cards	Armand	Arm Band
Abdullah	Ape Doll saying ah	Armando	A Mango
Abel	A Pill	Arnold	Arm Hold
Abraham	A Bra with Ham	Art	Art Work
Abram	A Broom	Arthur	Arthur Cartoon
Ace	Ace Card	Arturo	A Turtle
Adam	Atom	Ashton	Ton of Ashes
Adan	Apple Don (mob)	Atticus	Attic
Aden	A Den	August	A Gust
Adrian	A drain	Austin	Cowboy Boot (Texas)
Adriel	A drill	Avery	Ivory Tooth
Agustin	A Gust Tin Can	Axel	Ax
Ajay	A Jay (Jordan Shoe)	Barney	Barney
Al	Owl	Barrett	Rat in a Bar
Alan	Alan Wrench	Barry	Berry
Albert	Burnt Owl	Bart	Bart Simpson
Alberto	Burnt Toe	Bautista	Boat Taking Test
Alec	A Lick	Beckett	Bucket
Alejandro	Owl Hands Drying	Ben	Bench
Alessandro	A lasso in sand	Benjamin	Bench Jam
Alex	Owl that Licks	Bennett	Bent Net
Alexander	Owl Sander	Benny	Bending
Alexzander	Licking a Sander	Benson	Bending Sun
Alfonso	Owl Phone	Bently	Bentley Car
Alfred	Owl Fried	Bernard	St Bernard Dog
Ali	Muhammad Ali	Bernie	Burning Knee
Alonso	A Lasso	Bert	Bird
Alonzo	A Lasso Zebra	Bill	Duck's Bill
Alvin	Alvin (chipmunk)	Billy	Billy goat
Amare	A Mare	Blake	Bake Blade
Amir	A mirror	Bo	Bow Tie
Amos	A Moth	Bob	Bobsled
Andre	Hand Dry	Bobby	Bobby Pin
Andres	Ant wearing Dress	Boston	Ton of Busts
Andrew	Ants Drew	Brad	Bread
Andy	Ants Drinking Tea	Bradford	Bread in a Ford
Angel	Angel	Bradley	Bread with Leaves
Angelo	angel eating Jell-O	Brady	Braided hair
Anthony	ants in a tree	Brandon	Branded
Anton	Ton of Ants	Brendan	Braid Hen
Apollo	A stick (palo)	Brent	Brown Tent

MALE NAMES

Brett	Brat	Cliff	Cliff
Brian	Brain	Clifford	Clifford Dog
Brock	Brown Rock	Clint	Tint
Broderick	Brown Brick	Clinton	Ton of Lint
Bruce	Prune Juice	Clyde	Clydesdale horse
Bruno	Brown Nose	Cody	Code
Bud	Rose Bud	Colby	Cold Bee
Byron	Bicycle Running	Cole	Coal
Cameron	Camera	Coleman	Coleman Grill
Camilo	Camel Lost	Colin	Calling
Camron	Camel Running	Collin	Calling
Cannon	Cannon	Colt	Colt (Baby Horse)
Carl	Curl	Conner	Can of Nar
Carlos	Car Lace	Connor	Can of Nar
Carlton	Carton (Milk)	Conrad	Convict Rat
Carmelo	Caramel	Cooper	Chicken Coop
Carson	Car Son (little boy)	Corey	Apple Core
Carter	Charter a Boat	Cory	Apple Core
Cary	Carry	Craig	Crate
Case	Case (Briefcase)	Cristian	Christ
Casen	Case Net	Crosby	Crowbar
Casey	Case Yoyo	Cruz	Cruz Azul
Cash	Cash (ATM)	Curis	Curry Soup
Cason	Cat Gas On	Curt	Curtain
Ceasar	Julius Caesar	Curtis	Curtains Snake
Cecil	Seal	Dan	Dam
Cedric	Red Brick	Daniel	Downey (laundry)
Chad	ChapStick	Danny	Danish
Chance	Chance game	Dante	Diente (tooth with sombrero)
Chandler	Chandelier	Darrell	Barrel
Charles	Charcoal	Darren	Dart Run
Charlie	Charcoal Leaves	Darryl	Dog Barrel
Chase	Chase Credit Card	Dave	Cave
Chava	Guava	David	Bladed
Chester	Chest Drawers	Deacon	Bacon with D
Chet	Cheese Jet	Deandre	Tea Latte
Chris	Cross	Dennis	Dentist
Christian	Christ on Cross	Denzel	Denzel Washington
Christopher	Cross Gopher	Derek	Deer Brick
Chuck	Chalk	Derrick	Deer Brick
Clark	Clock	Dexter	Dexter's Laboratory
Claude	Cloud	Dick	Deck
Clay	Clay	Diego	Diego (Dora's)
Clayton	Ton of Clay	Dion	The On (light switch)

MALE NAMES

Dirk	Dirt	Fisher	Fisherman
Dominic	Dome Picnic	Fletcher	Fetcher
Dominick	Dominoes	Floyd	Flood
Don	Don	Francisco	Frank Sausage on Disco
Donald	Donald Duck	Franco	Frank Sausage O
Donovan	Dino Van	Frank	Frank Sausage
Doug	Dig	Frankie	Frank Sausage Envelope
Douglas	Dug a Glass	Franklin	Franklin Turtle
Drake	Drake rapper	Fred	Fried Egg
Drew	Drew	Freddy	Freddy Krueger
Duane	Drain	Frederick	Fried Brick
Dunking	Dunking	Gabriel	Gabble
Dustin	Dusting	Gael	Gargoyle
Dusty	Dust Powder	Gage	Gauge
Dwayne	The Rock	Garrett	Carrot
Dwight	White Dog	Gary	Garage
Dylan	Dill Pickle Ant	Geoffrey	Chef in a Tree
Earl	Pearl	George	Curious George
Ed	Head	Gerald	Chair that is Old
Eddie	Yeti	Gil	Fish Gil
Edgar	Head Gear	Gilbert	Gil Bird
Edmund	Head Mount	Giovanni	Cheeto Van Eye
Eduardo	Head Door	Giovanny	Cheeto Van
Edward	Head Wired	Glenn	Gluing
Edwin	Head and Wind	Gordon	Gordo (chubby)
Eli	Eel in Eye	Graham	Graham Crackers
Elon	Elephant Long	Grant	Granite (rock)
Emiliano	M&M Lion	Greg	Keg
Emilio	M&M Bolio (bread)	Guillermo	Guile vs Elmo
Emmanuel	Elephant manual	Gus	Gust of Wind
Emmitt	A Mitt	Gustavo	Gust Towel
Eric	Ear Ache	Hal	Hail
Erick	Ear Ache Kangaroo	Hank	Handkerchief
Ernesto	Ear Nest	Hans	Hands
Ernie	Ear and Knee	Harold	Old Hair
Erwin	Ear and Wind	Harry	Hair
Esteban	A Star in Van	Hector	Heckler
Ethan	Eating	Henry	Hen Rowing
Evan	Oven	Herb	Herb
Everette	Sever It	Herbert	Herb and Bird
Feibi	Frisbee	Homer	Homer Simpson
Felipe	Flip Elephant	Houston	Houston Rocket
Felix	Felix the Cat	Howard	How Indian
Fernando	Fern Ant	Hugh	Ewe

MALE NAMES

Hugo	Juice	Jon	Toilet
Hunter	Hunter	Jonah	Whale
Ian	Indian	Jonas	Jelly Donuts
Ignacio	Igloo Nacho	Jonathan	Toilet is Thin
Iman	Magnet (Spanish)	Jonathon	Toilet is Thin
Irv	Nerve	Jordan	Michael Jordan
Irving	Swerving	Jorge	Curious George juice
Isaac	Eye Sack	Jose	Hose (water)
Isayas	Ice Age	Joseph	Sloppy Joe on Sofa
Ismael	He's Smiling	Joshua	Shower
Ivan	Eye on Van	Josue	Shower Elephant
Jack	Car Jack	Juan	Wand
Jake	Cake	Jud	Jug
Jackson	Michael Jackson	Jude	Food
Jacob	Cake Cob (corn)	Julian	Jewel on Ant
Jaden	Skating J's (Jordan shoes)	Julio	Jewel Hanging
Jaime	Jamaica (Hibiscus tea)	Junior	June Bug
Jake	Shade	Justin	Just Do It Woosh
Jameer	Jam Deer	Keith	Keys
James	chains	Ken	Can
Jared	Chair Red	Kendrick	Can Brick
Jason	Jaybird in Sun	Kenneth	Can and Net
Javier	Javon (soap) Tire	Kent	Tent
Jay	Jaybird	Keshawn	Key Shine
Jeff	Chef in a Tree	Kevin	Cave Oven
Jeffrey	Geoffrey Giraffe	Kirk	Kick
Jeremiah	Cherry Jemima (syrup)	Klay	Clay Kangaroo
Jeremy	Cherry Mime	Kobe	Kobe Bryant
Jerimiah	Cherry Jemima (syrup) Ice	Kurt	Cut Curtain
Jerome	Chair Roam	Kyle	Tile
Jeronimo	Chair Dominoes	Lamar	Lace Mare
Jerry	Cherry	Lance	Sir Lancelot
Jess	Chest	Landry	Laundry
Jesse	Cheesy	Larry	Lariat
Jesus	Jesus	Lautaro	El Torro (the bull)
Jett	Jet	Lawrence	Law for Ants
Jim	Gym	Lebron	Lead brown
Jionni	Chonies (underwear)	Lee	Leaves
Joaquin	Joking Clown	Lemond	Lemon
Joe	Sloppy Joe Hamburger	Len	Lens
Joel	Jewel	Leo	Lion
Joey	Kangaroo	Leon	Lean On
John	Toilet	Leonardo	Lion with Nar (pomegranate)
Johnny	Chonies with Yoyo	Leroy	Lens in Toy

MALE NAMES

Les	Less Than Sign <	Morris	Morris The Cat
Levi	Levi Pants	Moses	Mud Roses
Lincoln	Lincoln	Nate	Nap Gate
Lionel	Lionel train	Nathan	Gnat
Livan	Levis Van	Neal	Nail
Lloyd	Lid	Ned	Ned Flanders
Lou	Blue	Nelson	Nail Sun
Lucas	Lucas Candy	Nick	Nickel
Luciano	I Love Lucy Ants	Nicolas	Nickel Gas
Luis	Lace	Nikola	Nikola Tesla
Luke	Luke Warm Water	Noah	No Air
Luther	Devil	Noel	Christmas Noel
Lyle	Aisle	Norman	Norseman
Mack	Mack Truck	Oliver	Olive
Manny	Man with Money	Omid	Ham Mud
Manuel	Manuel Book	Oscar	Academy award
Marcos	Markers with Snake	Otis	Otis Elevator
Marcus	Mucus	Owen	Owing
Mario	Super Mario	Pablo	Popsicle
Mark	Marker	Pat	Pat Something
Marlon	Marlin Nemo	Patricio	Patting Rice
Marshall	Law Enforcement	Patrick	St Patrick
Martin	Martian	Paul	Ball
Marvin	Carving	Pedro	Paid to Row
Mason	Mason Jar	Pete	Pete Moss
Mateo	Mat Boxeo	Peter	Peter cottontail
Matias	Mat Dice	Phil	Fill Up
Matt	Door Mat	Pierre	Pier
Matthew	Matt in a Pew	Preston	Pressing a Ton
Maurice	More Rice	Quincy	Wind and Sea
Mauricio	More Rice in O	Rafael	Roof Owl
Max	Mix	Rajon	Rat Toilet
Maximiliano	Mixing Mime Lion	Ralph	Raft
Maximo	Mix Mole	Ramiro	Ram with Mirror
Maxwell	Mix Well	Ramon	Ramon Noodles
Mel	Melon	Randal	Ran Doll
Melvin	Melt Van	Randall	Ran Doll Laser
Michael	Bicycle	Randolph	Ram with Dolphin
Mickey	Mickey Mouse	Randy	Ran Dice
Miguel	My Goal (soccer)	Ray	Ray of Light
Mike	Microphone	Raymond	Ray on a Mound
Miles	Miles	Reggie	Wrench Squeegee
Mitch	Mitt	Rex	T-Rex
Morgan	Organ	Ricardo	Recorder

MALE NAMES

Richard	Rich Yard	Sid	Sit
Richie	Dollar Sign	Simon	Simon Game
Rick	Brick	Spencer	Dispenser
Rob	Robber	Stan	A Stan
Robbie	Robe	Steve	Stove
Robert	Robot	Steven	Stove Oven
Rod	Rod	Stewart	Steward
Roderick	Rod in a Brick	Stu	Stew
Rodney	Rod in Knee	Sylvester	Sylvester Cat
Rodrigo	Rod Rug	Tad	Tadpole
Rogelio	Row of Jell-O	Tansel	Utensil
Roger	Rod in Chair	Ted	Ted Bear Dead
Roland	Rolling	Teddy	Teddy Bear
Roman	Roman Soldier	Terry	Tearing an Envelope
Ron	Rabbit Run	Tex	Texas
Ronald	Ronald McDonald	Theodore	Teeth on Door
Ronnie	Running	Thomas	Thermos
Ross	Boss	Tim	Tin Can
Rowan	Rowing	Timothy	Tin of Tea
Roy	Roy Rogers	Toby	Toe and Bee
Ruben	Ruben Sandwich	Todd	Toad
Rudolph	Rudolph Red Nose	Tom	Tom Cat
Russ	Rusts	Tomas	Dome with snakes
Russell	Rustle	Tommy	Tommy gun
Ryan	Sea Lion	Tony	Tony the Tiger
Ryder	Bike Rider	Tracy	Tracing with Stencil
Sam	Uncle Sam	Trevor	Tree Beaver
Sammy	Uncle Sam on knee	Troy	Troy Movie
Samuel	Uncle Sam on mule	Ty	Tie
Sandy	Sand	Tyler	Tire
Santiago	Saint Eating Eggo	Tyrese	Tie Rose
Santino	Saint on Dinosaur	Tyrone	Tie Rowing
Santos	Multiple Saints	Tyson	Mike Tyson
Saul	Salt	Valentino	Valentine Card
Scott	Scott paper towels	Van	Van
Sean	Shark Yawning Envelope	Vern	Fern
Sebastian	Sebastian the Crab	Vernon	Furry Nun
Sergio	Surge Protector	Vic	Vick's cough drop
Seymour	See More	Vicente	Fence with Sombrero
Shane	Shine	Victor	Flick Door
Shawn	Shark Yawning	Vince	Fence
Sheldon	Shielding	Vincent	Fencing
Sherman	German Shepard	Wade	Wade in Pool
Sid	Sit	Wallace	Walrus

MALE NAMES

Walter	Cup of Water	
Ward	Wart	
Warren	Warden	
Wayne	Rain	
Willie	Free Willy Whale	
Winston	Wind Ton	

FEMALE NAMES

Aaliyah	Owl Idea (light Bulb)	Audrey	Laundry
Abby	A Bee	Autumn	Leaves
Abigail	A bee in a pail	Barbara	Barbed Wire
Ada	A Doll	Beatrice	Beat Rice
Adell	A Bell	Becky	Horse Bucking
Adriana	A Drain	Belinda	Bee Lint
Agustina	A Gust	Bernadette	Burn a Net
Alejandra	Owl Hands Drying	Bernice	Burn Dice (on fire)
Alessandra	A Lasso in Sand	Bessie	Beso (kiss)
Alice	Lice	Beth	Bath
Alicia	Owl Shield	Bethany	Bath Tub Knee
Alise	Owl Shoelace	Betty	Betting
Allison	Lice in the sun	Beverly	Bed of Leaves
Allysa	A Lasso	Bianca	Binaca (mouth spray)
Allyson	A Lice Sun yoyo	Billie	Billy Goat
Alma	Owl mom	Blanca	White
Alondra	A Laundry	Bobbie	Fishing Bobber
Amanda	A Man and Dog	Bonnie	Bonnet
Amber	Flame	Brenda	Brand New Dog
Amelia	Email (envelope)	Briana	Brain
Amy	Aiming	Bridget	Bridges
Ana	Ant Apple	Britney	Britney Spears
Andrea	Ant Drinking Water	Brooklyn	Brakes
Angel	Angel	Camila	Camel Lace
Angela	Jell-O	Camille	Camel
Angelica	Angel Cuffs	Candice	Can of Dice
Angelina	Angelina Jolie	Candy	Candy
Angie	Algae	Carla	Car with Lace
Anilette	A Knee Lid	Carmen	Car and Man
Anita	Kneading	Carol	Carol
Ann	Ant	Carol	Christmas Carol
Annabelle	Ant Bell	Carolina	Carolina Panther
Annette	A Net	Carolyn	Caroling Lint
Annie	Orphan Annie	Carrie	Carry
Antonia	Ant Toe Nail	Catalina	Catalina Island
April	A Pill	Catherine	Cat Running
Ariana	Ariana Grande	Celeste	Cell Phone Stars
Ariel	Mermaid	Celia	Cell Phone
Arlene	Ark Lean	Charlotte	Spider Web
Ashley	Ashes	Chelsea	Shell See
Ashlyn	Ash Violin	Cheryl	Chair that is Ill
Astrid	Ostrich	Chloe	Clover
Athena	Athena Goddess	Chris	Cross
Aubrey	I Breath(elizer)	Chrissy	Cross in the Sea

FEMALE NAMES

Christine	Christmas tree	Faith	Church
Cristine	Cross in Stone	Fatima	Fat Mouse
Cicely	Sister Silly	Felicia	Fleece
Cindy	Cinnamon Candy	Fernanda	Fern Ant
Claire	Clear Eyes	Florence	Flour Rinse
Clara	Clarinet	Frances	Eiffel Tower
Claudia	Cloud	Gabriela	Gable Roof
Colleen	Calling	Gabrielle	Gabrielle Olympics
Connie	Convict	Gaby	Cabbie
Crystal	Crystal Vase	Gail	Gale Force Winds
Cynthia	Cinder Block	Genece	Jean Knees
Dakota	Duck Coat	Genesis	Jean Sister
Daniela	Downey Lace	Georgia	Gorge
Daphne	Dolphin	Gina	Greener
Darlene	Door with Beans	Ginger	Ginger Bread Man
Dawn	Dawn	Ginny	Bottle of Gin on Knees
Debbie	Dead Bee	Giselle	Chisel
Deborah	Dead Boar	Giuliana	Glue
Debra	Deer Zebra	Glenda	Blender
Delanda	Dell Comp. on Land	Gloria	Old Glory
Denise	Disease	Grace	Saying a Prayer
Desiree	Dessert	Gris	Grease oil
Destiny	Desk Tiny	Guadalupe	Guacamole Loop
Diana	Dying Ants	Hannah	Hand
Dixie	Confederate Flag	Harper	Harp
Donna	Donald Duck	Harriet	Lariat
Doris	Doors	Hattie	Hat
Dorothy	Door Teeth	Hazel	Hazelnut Ice-cream
Dottie	Dots	Heather	Feather
Edna	Head Nut	Heaven	Oven
Eileen	Eye Leaning	Heidi	Hiding
Elaine	Airplane	Helen	Halo Melon
Eleanor	Plane Landing on Door	Hilda	Hold Apple
Elise	A Lease	Holly	Boughs of Holly
Elizabeth	Lizard Breath	Hope	Hop over Rope
Ellen	Island	Ida	Idaho Potato
Ellie	Smelly	Irene	Eye Ring
Emily	Family	Iris	A Wrist
Emma	Email	Irma	Ear Muff
Erica	Ear	Isabel	Ice Bell
Erin	Earing	Isabelle	Ice Bell Lion
Eva	Evil (horns)	Ivy	Poison Ivy
Eve	Eve Paws	Jackie	Car Jack
Evelyn	Violin	Jacqueline	Lint on a Jack

FEMALE NAMES

Jade	Jade stone	Laura	Laurels
Jamie	Chain on Knees	Lauren	Laurel Run
Jan	Jam	Laurie	Lowering Crane
Jane	Jane Tarzan	Layla	Lay Down
Janet	Jam in a Net	Leslie	Less than Sign <
Janice	Jam Ice	Lexi	Flexing
Jazmin	Jasmine Princess	Lillian	Lily with Ants
Jean	Jeans	Lily	Lily flower
Jeanette	Jeans in a Net	Linda	Lion Dog Leash
Jeanie	Genie	Lindsey	Lint See
Jennifer	Chin Fur	Lisa	Mona Lisa
Jenny	Chimney	Liz	Lizard
Jessica	Chest with Cuffs	Lois	Lace
Jill	Pill	Lola	Lollipop
Jo	Sloppy Joe Burger	Loretta	Lobo Beretta
Joan	Joan of Arc	Lori	Loar Guitar
Joanne	Sloppy Joe w/ ants	Lorraine	Low Rain
Jocelyn	Chest Lint	Louise	Low Easel
Joy	Joy dishwashing liquid	Luana	Luna (moon) apple
Joyce	Juice	Lucille	Loose Sail
Juanita	One Knee	Lucinda	Loose Rope on Cinder Block
Judith	Chew Desk	Lucy	I Love Lucy
Judy	Judge Judy	Luna	Luna (moon)
Julia	Jewel Apple	Lupe	Loop (earing)
Juliana	Jewel Ant Apple	Lydia	Lid
Julie	Jewelry	Lynn	Lint
Juliet	Jewel Net	Madeline	Mad at Lint
June	June Bug	Mae	Mayo
Kaitlyn	Kite LInt	Maggie	Maggie's Pacifier (Simpsons)
Karen	Carrot	Mandy	Mandolin
Kassandra	Case Sand	Marcy	Marching
Kate	Gate	Margaret	Market
Katherine	Cat that Runs	Margarita	Margarita Drink
Kathleen	Cat that Leans	Marge	Marge Simpson Hair
Kathy	Cat Teeth	Maria	Sangria Wine
Katie	Kite	Marian	Mare with Ants
Kay	Key	Marianne	Marry Ant
Kelly	Surfboard (Kelly Slater)	Marie	Mare
Kendra	Can Draw	Marilyn	Marry Lint
Khloe	Clover (Kangaroo)	Marina	Marry Run
Kim	Climb	Marissa	Marry Seesaw
Kimberly	Swim Bear	Marjorie	My Jury
Kirsten	Skirt Stem	Marlene	Mare Lean
Latoya	Lace on Toy	Marry Ellen	Marry a Melon

FEMALE NAMES

Marsha	Marshmallow	Peg	Peg
Martha	Vineyard	Peggy	Peg Yoyo
Mary	Merry Go Round	Penny	Penny Coin
Megan	Mayo Bacon	Phyllis	Philly
Melanie	Melon on Knee	Priscilla	Pass the Jell-O
Melissa	Molasses	Rachel	Ray Shining on a Shell
Meredith	Mare in a Dish	Ramona	Ram Moaning
Michelle	Shell Sleeping (mimi)	Rebecca	Rope Deck
Mikayla	Milk Laugh	Renee	Raining Elephants
Mila	Miel (Honey)	Roberta	Robot
Minnie	Minnie Mouse	Robin	Bird
Miriam	Mirror Ham	Rochelle	Rowing Shells
Mitzi	Mitt that can See	Rocio	Rice O
Molly	Mole	Rosa	Rose (Red)
Mona	Moaning	Rosalie	Rose Leaves (Pedals)
Monica	Harmonica	Rosalyn	Rose Lint
Monique	Money Kangaroo	Rose	Rose (White)
Morgan	Organ	Rosie	Rosie Blush
Mya	Mime Apple	Roxanne	Rocks in Hand
Nan	Nun	Ruth	Baby Ruth candy bar
Nancy	Nun Eating Seeds	Sadie	Saddle
Naomi	Knight Mime	Sally	Salad
Natalia	Net Telly (TV) w/ Apple	Samantha	Saw man
Natalie	Net Telly (TV)	Sandra	Sander
Nellie	Kneeling	Sandy	Sand
Nicole	Nickel	Sarah	Sarah Lee cup cakes
Nina	Knee	Sasha	Sash
Nirey	Knee Crown (rey)	Scarlett	Scar Lid
Nora	Snoring	Selena	Selling Cash Register
Noreen	No Rain	Serena	Tennis Racket (Williams)
Norma	Normal (gauge)	Sharon	Sharing
Olive	Olives	Sheila	Shield
Olivia	Oh Liver!	Shelley	Shells
Paige	Page (paper)	Sherry	Bottle of Sherry
Pam	Spam	Sheryl	Shirt that is Ill
Pamela	Paneling	Shirley	Shirt Sleeves
Paris	Parrot	Sidney	Sit on Knee
Pat	Act of Patting	Sky	Blue Sky
Patricia	Pats of Butter	Sofia	Sofa
Patty	Hamburger Patty	Sonia	Sony Walkman
Paula	Polo	Sophia	Sew a Bee
Paulina	Pole Leaning on Apple	Stacy	Stacy Adams Shoes
Pauline	Pole that Leans	Stephanie	Step on Knees
Pearl	Pearl	Sue	Suit

FEMALE NAMES

Sue Ann	Suit with Ants
Summer	Hot Sun
Susan	Lazy Susan
Susannah	Snoozing hand
Susie	Snoozing
Suzanne	Snoozing Ant
Sylvia	Silverware
Tammy	Tummy
Tanya	Tan Yoyo
Teresa	Tree Saw
Terry	Terry Cloth
Tess	Test
Tracy	Tracing Stencil
Valentina	Valentine Card
Valeria	Valet Guy
Valerie	Library
Vanessa	van wearing a dress
Velma	Velma Glasses
Veronica	Violin Harmonica
Vicky	Vick's cough drops
Victoria	Victory Trophy
Viki	Vicks Vaporub
Virginia	Fur Genie
Vivian	Bib on Van
Wanda	Wand
Wendy	Wendy's Pigtails
Wilma	Wilma Flintstone
Windy	Wind
Yesenia	Yellow Sony CD player
Yvette	Corvette
Yvonne	Eve Van (dog van)
Zoe	Sewing
Zoey	Zoo animals

THANK YOU

THANK YOU GOD for ALL OF YOUR BLESSINGS and for DIRECTING ME TO ALL OF THESE PEOPLE in MY LIFE!

1. **My Mom!** Yesenia Emeria Carrion! As a teenager, she came here as an illegal immigrant from Mexico. She risked her life to make sure that her future kids didn't have to go through all of the struggles that she went through as a young girl. Between the ages of 4-16, she would be working out in the corn fields from sunrise to sunset. Walking barefoot 2 hours one way and 2 hours back. She saw the pain that her kids were going to have to endure if she decided to stay back and raise a family in Mexico and made the tough choice of leaving my grandparents and aunts behind so that she could raise her future kids in "El Norte" (up North, The USA). If it wasn't for her bold decision to make that move, I wouldn't be doing what I'm doing now. Te Quiero Much Ma!

2. **Feibi Liu**. This gentleman saw an 18 year old kid from the hood struggling and decided to give him a chance at taking his life to a whole new level. He opened my eyes to an entirely different world of endless possibilities. He pushed me to pass any limitations that I had set for myself. He has been a big brother, mentor, and one of my best friends throughout the last several years! Thank you bro!

3. **Dion Jaffee**. He has been instrumental at connecting me with the right people to get me to the point where I am at now. If it wasn't for him helping me out when I was 20 years old and in a very bad place mentally, I would not be in this field of memory. He has done so much for me throughout the last several years and I owe him tremendously for everything! Thanks bro! We're going to do big things!

4. **Ron White**. What can I say about this guy. I found out about the 2x USA Memory Champion, Ron White, because Dion saw him present the memory techniques at a seminar. When I was in need of a mentor to get me out of my mental slump, Ron was the one that pulled me out. He not only has helped me improve my memory, Ron has also helped me improve my students ability to memorize and learn information much more quickly through his business mentoring! Gracias Amigo for everything! Hope to share the stage with you soon.

5. **To my future daughter!** Just like my mom saw her future kids growing up in a much better environment than where she grew up, I see my future daughter growing up in a place where she can truly go after her goals, dreams, ambitions, and aspirations without anything or anyone holding her back. I want to set an example for her that everything that she wants to accomplish, she will be able to do. My daughter will have an incredible childhood full of experiences, adventures, fun, laughter, growth, and a loving family to support her every step of the way. Baby girl, you aren't here right now, but trust me when I say this, I'm thinking about you every single second of the day! You are my biggest driving factor towards me going after what I want to in order to leave a lasting legacy for you to be proud of. Baby girl, I can't wait to hold you in my arms. Believe me, I will work extremely hard from this point forward to make sure that you have an amazing life! Your mama, grandma, grandpa, aunts, uncles, and cousins, can't wait to see you.

MORE THANK YOU's AND SHOUTOUTS

Family:

- My Bros Christian and Chava
- My Sisters Gris and Monique
- My Nieces Alise and Allyson
- Carlos and Albert

Friends:

- Gilbert Delgado
- Daniel J Jackson
- Jaime Michel
- Nick Rave
- Nelson Dellis (www.climbformemory.com),
- Brad Zupp (www.exceptionalassemblies.com)
- Johnny Briones
- GYLS Fam: Juan, Omid, Nick, Sergio, Adriana, etc...

And Thank You to everyone else who has helped me out along the way!

LEARN MORE/CONTACT

Learn more about Luis Angel's **"Better Memory Now"** programs and other Memory Training material for Professionals, Students, Memory Athletes, and Everyone Else, by going to:

www.AEMind.com

SOCIAL

YT: Youtube.com/aemind
FB: Facebook.com/aemind1
IG: ae.mind
Twitter: @aemind

Email: Support@AEMind.com